Dear Sheila

Figure 1 - Jerri Tuck

Love in Christ
Just Jerri

JUST JERRI

... And He said to them: Follow Me, and I will make you fishers of men" –
Matthew 4:19

By

Jerri Tuck

TRIBNET PUBLICATIONS

SACRAMENTO, CALIFORNIA

Just Jerri

TRIBNET PUBLICATIONS

SACRAMENTO, CALIFORNIA

PRINTED IN THE UNITED STATES OF AMERICA

WWW.TRIBNET.ORG

© COPYRIGHT JERRI TUCK, 2017

ISBN-13:978-1548599881
ISBN-10:1548599883

ALL IMAGES FROM WIKIPEDIA COMMONS, PUBLIC DOMAIN - UNLESS OTHERWISE NOTED

EXTERIOR COVER DESIGN BY DOUGLAS W. KRIEGER

ALL SCRIPTURE TAKEN FROM THE NEW KING JAMES VERSION OF THE BIBLE UNLESS OTHERWISE NOTED

Table of Contents

Table of Figures vii

Dedication x

Acknowledgements xi

Preface xii

Foreword: By Douglas W. Krieger xv

   Week 1 – Living the Dash 3

   Week 2 - Tradition 7

   Week 3 – Signs of the Times 11

   Week 4 – Are You up to the Challenge? 15

   Week 5 – Are We There Yet? 19

   Week 6 – Are You Drifting? 23

   Week 7 – A Journey's End – A Tribute to Don Morsey ... 27

   Week 8 – What Train? 31

   Week 9 – Finding The Rainbow 35

   Week 10 – Dressed for the Occasion 39

   Week 11 – Needle in a Haystack 43

   Week 12 – All Roads Lead to Where? 47

   Week 13 - Vision Problems 51

   Week 14 - Forever Stamp 55

   Week 15 - I Know How They Buck Now 59

   Week 16 - Old Age is Curious 63

   Week 17 - Going Once, Going Twice . . . SOLD! 67

   Week 18 - Joy in the Journey 71

   Week 19 - Love Letters 75

   Week 20 - The World is a Dangerous Place 79

Week 21 - An Appointment with Death.................................83
Week 22 - Bingo..87
Week 23 - Cast Your Bread Upon the Waters.......................93
Week 24 - Are You For Real?...99
Week 25 - Do You Have A Beeper? 103
Week 26 - The Future Looks Good......................................107
Week 27 - God's 800 Number..111
Week 28 - Let Us Pray 115
Week 29 - The Blessings Continue......................................119
Week 30 - The Ultimate Rip-Off..123
Week 31 - Donors Needed...127
Week 32 - Mystery House 131
Week 33 - No Greater Love 135
Week 34 - Playing Cupid 139
Week 35 - Words to Live By..143
Week 36 - The Last Reservation..146
Week 37 - Modern-Day Esthers 151
Week 38 - A Divided House...155
Week 39 - Why A Bible Reading Marathon........................161
Week 40 - More Than a Case of Spilled Milk......................167
Week 41 - I'm Standing on the Inside.................................171
Week 42 - Buried in Time..175
Week 43 - Where The Tree Falls...181
Week 44 - Happy Birthday Bertha!....................................185
Week 45 - The Rocks Will Cry Out!....................................189
Week 46 - Legal or Moral?...193

Week 47 - Nothing New Under the Sun *199*
Week 48 - But Wait, There's More! *203*
Week 49 - Are You Superstitious *207*
Week 50 - Seasons of Life *211*
Week 51 - Unseen Footprints *215*
Week 52 - Writing Our Autobiography *221*

About the Author *227*

Other Books by Jerri Tuck *231*

Tables of Figures

Figure 1 - Jerri Tuck i
Figure 2 - Have You Heard the Good News? x
Figure 3 – Jerri with Doug & Charlie xi
Figure 4 - Charlie Tuck- For Bleckley Co. Commissioner! xii
Figure 5 - Judy Sherling xiii
Figure 6 - Jerri at Retreat Book Table 2
Figure 7 - Checking the Dates 4
Figure 8 - Tradition #1 8
Figure 9 - Tradition #2 9
Figure 10 - Signs of the Times 12
Figure 11 - Riding with the Hell's Angels 16
Figure 12 - Are We There Yet? 20
Figure 13 - Are We There Yet? 24
Figure 14 - A Tribute to Don Morsey 29
Figure 15 - What Train? 31
Figure 16 - Finding the Rainbow 36
Figure 17 - Dressed for the Occasion 40
Figure 18 - Needle in a Haystack 44
Figure 19 - The Road Less Traveled 46
Figure 20 - All Roads Lead to Where? 47
Figure 21 – The Colors Tell the Story 52
Figure 22 - Forever Stamp 55
Figure 23 – I Know How They Buck Now 60
Figure 24 - Reaching Higher No Matter What! 62
Figure 25 – The Tucks as Mr. & Mrs. Noah 64
Figure 26 - Going Once, Going Twice . . . SOLD! 67
Figure 27 - Going Once, Going Twice . . . SOLD! 68
Figure 28 - Joy in the Journey 72
Figure 29 - Ecclesiastes 9:10 74
Figure 30 - Love Letters 76
Figure 31 - The World is a Dangerous Place 80
Figure 32 – An Appointment with Death 84
Figure 33 - The Miracle of the Scarlet Thread - Bingo! 87

Figure 34 - The Miracle of the Scarlet Thread #2 89
Figure 35 - The Honor of Kings to Search out a Matter.......... 92
Figure 36 - Cast Your Bread Upon the Waters 94
Figure 37 - Are You for Real?.. 99
Figure 38 – WARNING: Low Fuel! 104
Figure 39 – Grit Newsboy 107
Figure 40 - God's 800 Number 112
Figure 41 – Monument to Slain Kids.................................... 117
Figure 42 - The Blessings Continue 120
Figure 43 – Bernie Madoff.. 124
Figure 44 – Charlie & Cousin Dorma Westlotorn 128
Figure 45 - Mystery House.. 132
Figure 46 - No Greater Love 136
Figure 47 – Wade & Bonnie Conklin 140
Figure 48 – Words Can Hurt 144
Figure 49 – Dillon & Katie Kestner – Wedding Day 148
Figure 50 – Martyr – Neda Agha-Soltan 151
Figure 51 - Modern-Day Esthers... 152
Figure 52 - A Strong Mountaineer 155
Figure 53 - Alan & Charlie.. 156
Figure 54 - There's no division here! 157
Figure 55 - The Bible Reading Marathon 161
Figure 56 – ACLJ – Andy Ekonomou 162
Figure 57 -Mayor Pro-Tem Willie Basby 163
Figure 58 – BRM Volunteer-Buddy G.W. Roberson............ 167
Figure 59 – BRM Volunteer-Jim Parks 168
Figure 60 – BCLC Pres. Don Giles....................................... 169
Figure 61 – All Cleaned Up 172
Figure 62 – Right Back Into The Mud 173
Figure 63 - The Bomb at the Railroad Yard 175
Figure 64 - Charlie & Jerri at former home in CA 176
Figure 65 – Downed Trees Everywhere 181
Figure 66 – A Brand New Look.. 182
Figure 67 - Happy Birthday Bertha! 185

Figure 68 – Victory Through the Blood 186
Figure 69 – Pro-Lifers at Mt. Rushmore 189
Figure 70 – Rocks by Martha Lee Francis 190
Figure 71 - Jerri's Mom, Pauline 193
Figure 72 - Jerri (middle) L-Doug - R-Dwight Bros. 194
Figure 73 - The Gift of God 195
Figure 74 – Horrific Texts On Cell Phones Today 199
Figure 75 – There Is Forgiveness with God 200
Figure 76 - Ron Popeil - But There's More! 203
Figure 77 – Save Your Fork! 204
Figure 78 - "666" - How did this Happen? 207
Figure 79 - Officer Carlos Altamirano Gets VeriChip 208
Figure 80 – Aunt Carrie Tuck 211
Figure 81 - The Tuck Farm House in Georgia 212
Figure 82 - Bob Allen 215
Figure 83 - Footprints in the Sand 216
Figure 84 – Wedding Day with Jerri's Parents 222
Figure 85 – Autobiography for Tuck Kids 223
Figure 86 – So Many Stories Preserved 225
Figure 87 - Charlie & Jerri Tell Their Story 227
Figure 88 - The Cochran Journal, Cochran, GA 230
Figure 89 - GONE FISHIN' by Jerri Tuck 231
Figure 90 - Cochran Journal's Stories on BRM 233
Figure 91 - PATCHWORK FAMILY by Jerri Tuck 235

Dedication

This book is lovingly dedicated to the memory of

Don Morsey

(A Man Who Unceasingly Shared the Good News!)

Figure 2 - Have You Heard the Good News?

ACKNOWLEDGEMENTS

I am so blessed to have a husband like Charlie and a brother like Doug Krieger. These two men have been the backbone of my third book, *Just Jerri*. Like Aaron and Hur of old who supported Moses on the mountain, these two have likewise lifted my arms as I grew faint in the undertaking. They have encouraged and pushed me until I thought I couldn't type another line, but the work has been completed and I'm thrilled to share some of my favorite *Just Jerri* stories with you.

For several years my husband had encouraged me to compile some of my favorite *Just Jerri* weekly columns into a devotional book, but I always had one excuse after another why I didn't have time . . . or I wasn't inspired . . . or it was too much work. Truly, 'two are better than one and a three-fold cord is not quickly broken' (Ecclesiastes 4:9, 12). Between the three of us (and the LORD), we got it done.

I pray this 52-week devotional will bless and encourage you. It has been written with much thought and prayer. Each story, along with daily devotional thoughts and Scripture references will challenge you in your walk with the Lord.

Figure 3 – Jerri with Doug & Charlie

PREFACE

In 1997 my precious husband decided to make a run for the office of Bleckley County Commissioner. The current commissioner was retiring and this was a special election. I was so proud of him and I knew he would do a fantastic job if elected.

Charlie had been the Bleckley County Tax Assessor for the past five years and also had initiated the first Bleckley County Building Code in our community. There was no doubt that Charlie knew the county inside and out. Who better to help our county?

Figure 4 - Charlie Tuck- For Bleckley Co. Commissioner!

As his wife, I was determined to back him with everything in me. In fact, our whole family got caught up in the 1997 special election and we were his biggest fans and supporters.

In addition to running ads and wearing tee-shirts advertising, "Charlie Tuck for Bleckley County Commissioner," we

Preface

also had signs printed up, which I personally installed around the county at strategic intersections.

Not just trusting in our physical efforts, I took to my knees in fervent prayer. Every Monday I devoted myself to fasting and praying for God's will in the election. *

While in prayer one day I *heard* a voice saying, "Judy Sherling (editor of our local newspaper, The Cochran Journal) is going to ask you to write a weekly column and you're to tell her yes!" What???

That had nothing to do with the price of tea in China and I was absolutely sure that, either I made up that thought, or the Devil put it into my head. I promptly discarded that thought, saying to myself, "Where did that come from? I'm too busy to write a weekly column!"

Figure 5 - Judy Sherling

About a week later I walked into the newspaper office to bring an ad for Charlie's election campaign. I had spoken just a few minutes to the receptionist, when running breathlessly from the newsroom into the reception area, came Judy!

"Jerri," she said with a big smile, "How about writing a weekly column for the paper?"

You guessed it. With my jaw dropping, I looked at her and said, "Sure!" What else could I say? I can tell you I walked out of that office absolutely stunned. The exact words that God told me, Judy would say to me; she had just spoken!

Thus, began the 20 years of me writing the *Just Jerri* column for both the Cochran Journal and the Twiggs New Era.

It has been a great journey and has been a source of amazement to me personally, that the Lord gives me ideas every week about what I am to write.

A few years ago, Charlie started encouraging me to compile some of these weekly columns into a book. His thought was that these articles would not only preserve some of the best *Just Jerri* articles for posterity, but would also encourage readers if it was in a weekly devotional format.

The 52 *Just Jerri* columns, one for every week of the year, are followed by daily Scriptures pertinent to each article with declarations we can make to encourage each of us in our Christian lives.

It is my prayer that these stories and Scriptures will help you enjoy a life of victory and abundance in every situation you may be facing.

*Oh, by the way. God did have His will accomplished, just as we prayed. Charlie did NOT win the election. I guess you figured out, just like I did; no one is going to vote for the tax man!

Jerri Tuck

Cochran, Georgia

FOREWORD

By
Douglas W. Krieger

FIFTY-TWO WEEKS AWAIT THE READER –IT'S REALLY A JOURNEY OF *JUST JERRI* IN PURSUIT OF SOULS . . . souls who will hear the Good News because Jesus said, "I will make you fishers of men."

Jerri's journey has taken her to some unbelievable places—meeting literally thousands along the way. Little did she know that the day she surrendered her life to her Lord Jesus that He had planned such a venture that would lead her around the world in sharing the GOOD NEWS–the Good News that liberated her from the penalty of sin into a "New Creature" in her Deliverer—her Savior . . . for the Spirit of Christ was now within this vessel under mandate to fulfill the Great Commission to tell the world of God's relentless love and grace!

From Hell's Angel to God's Messenger—Jerri Tuck broke free into the arms of Jesus Who rescued her from the brink of catastrophe to become His witness of life out of death, of eternal beauty for the ashes of this world.

We're pleased here at Tribnet to continue this series of personal evangelism and of God's supernatural intervention into the lives of so many through a vessel committed to the One Who is the Captain of her salvation.

There are many testimonials included in this initial volume . . . many, and/or most of the stores contained in **JUST JERRI** were published in local Newspapers in Central Georgia, USA, under the banner of *JUST JERRI*—true human-interest stories of God's love and salvation.

Jerri knew from the very beginning as a young person at the age of 15 that she could not stop sharing the Good News!

Good News to all who would or would not listen . . . her job was to sow the seed of Life into all sorts of ground . . . some hardened their hearts; but others were so ready to hear the "Words of Life" and, as Jerri was, burst forth into Life . . . they were born from above as she was and commenced their own journey in growing in the grace of God.

Along the way there have been scores of people some desperate, some indifferent, and some *JUST JERRI* material. All seen by Jerri as incredibly valuable to her Lord and Savior. We hope you will enjoy this blessed accounting of real life stories and impressions from Jerri's pen—may they stir your spirit to be a true witness and testimony of God's love to a world so truly in need of the Savior.

Douglas W. Krieger, *Jerri's brother*

Sacramento, California,

July 2017 www.tribnet.org

JUST JERRI

By

Jerri Tuck

Figure 6 - Jerri at Retreat Book Table

Week 1
LIVING THE DASH

I'm not sure where I first heard or read the phrase, "If you read your Bible hit and miss, you'll miss more than you hit," but the words truly resonated deep inside me. Consistent, methodical Bible reading is a sure-fire way to get to know God and be prepared for life's eventualities.

The New Year looms before us with unknown challenges, opportunities and perhaps trials never before encountered. We can rest assured that nothing will be a surprise to the Lord. We are reassured over and over that "known unto God are all His works from the beginning of the world" (Acts 15:18).

Each day we are writing a chapter in the biography of our life. The Lord knows the ending, while we are only learning the plot on a day by day basis. The only thing in which we have assurance is the final destination of our souls.

Unlike the cartoon depicting a terrorist who woke up in hell saying, "You mean I don't get 72 virgins?" (From the LA Times, by political cartoonist, Michael Ramirez); we can count on the absolute integrity of God when He promises a home in Heaven for those who have put their trust in the Son of His love.

Many years ago, a friend of mine spent a week with the family of President Gerald Ford as they shared in the grief of his passing. I knew President Ford as a president, but never as an intimate friend. I wasn't surprised one bit when I wasn't invited to his Southern California home.

At one time my friend and his wife were next door neighbors with Gerald and Betty Ford. They shared meals together, enjoyed hobbies with one another and celebrated mutual anniversaries together. It was no wonder that during a time of sadness they were together again.

Enjoying the company of a former president would be a unique experience. It's hard for me to imagine just hanging out with the Ford family on a golf course or a race track, yet for my friend it was as natural as me meeting with my friends. They had a wonderful relationship, a family-type relationship.

For those who don't want anything to do with the Lord there will come a time when they won't have to worry about Christians extending invitations to church, bible studies or special meetings to learn about God.

More succinctly, the gentle voice of the Holy Spirit who keeps prompting them to turn away from their sin and come into a relationship with God will be silenced forever. Friend, you who don't want anything to do with God or His Word, rest assured a time is coming when all those invitations to come into a relationship with God will cease.

Today God isn't inviting you to a state funeral of a passing dignitary, He is inviting you into a living relationship with His Son, who died and rose from the grave.

Figure 7 - Checking the Dates

When Osama Bin Laden left this earth from a bloody spray of bullets he was only one second into eternity when he realized his entire life had been mistakenly lived.

The misguided terrorist was sincere in his beliefs, but he was sincerely wrong. His threats and tirades may continue to be republished on YouTube and Islamists social networks, but if he could give out the truth, it would not be: "Death to America and Israel!"

I believe Bin Laden's message would be to, "Look to the Living God, who alone can give you life and immortality."

Life is a preparation for eternity. Friend, you were designed by an Omnipotent Creator to live forever in Heaven or Hell. The time between your birth and your death is but a dash. Look at the tombstones in a nearby cemetery. The dates are only separated by a dash. That's all we get folks . . . just a dash and we are gone.

If you're looking for a New Year's resolution that will make a difference in your life, try reading the Bible every day. That, plus a relationship with the living God, will do more to make your life worth living than any amount of personal assets you can acquire, more than trimming your weight to be a perfect "10" or checking off reading everything on the NY Times Best Sellers' List.

Remember, all you have is a dash from your beginning to your end on this earth. How will you spend your dash in the coming year?

SCRIPTURES FOR MEDITATION

(Selah – think on these things)

MONDAY: *I will commit my life to Christ one day at a time.*

Scriptures: Deuteronomy 33:25b; Psalms 90:12, 119:105; Isaiah 30:21; Luke 9:62; James 4:13-15.

TUESDAY: *I will seek the Lord's will in all that I do.*

Scriptures: I Samuel 16:7; Psalms 1:1-3; Proverbs 3:5-6, 19:21; Philippians 1:10.

WEDNESDAY: *I will commit to reading my guidebook, the Bible, every day.*

Scriptures: Joshua 1:8; I Kings 8:56; Psalms 19:7-8, 63:1, 119:97; Matthew 24:35.

THURSDAY: *I will remember that the Lord is with me every moment of every day.*

Scriptures: Deuteronomy 20:4; Isaiah 46:4, 52:12; Zechariah 8:23; Matthew 28:20; John 16:7; Hebrews 13:5-6.

FRIDAY: *I will remember that the things of this earth are temporal.*

Scriptures: Genesis 5:21-24; I Samuel 12:18-23; Ecclesiastes 3:1-11; 2 Corinthians 4:18; 2 Corinthians 5:1-6.

SATURDAY: *I will make my life count for eternity.*

Scriptures: Proverbs 4:1-4; Matthew 25:34-40; I Corinthians 3:11-15; Revelation 4:1-4, 21:1-7.

Week 2
TRADITION

Although Christmas is in the past and New Year celebrations are but a memory, I'm still overwhelmed with all the decorations scattered everywhere that have to be collected, organized and stored away.

Every year we go through this. I want to cut back on decorations and Charlie feels it's a tradition, arguing the grandchildren need to enjoy all the lights and other paraphernalia. I'm beginning to think he's related to Topol. In *Fiddler on the Roof*, Topol, a poor Jewish peasant, dramatically waves his forefinger and sings, "*Tradition.*" No matter what, we must have tradition!

One of the traditions we've always celebrated is the New Year's dinner of corned beef and cabbage. This tradition, handed down from Charlie's hillbilly relatives in West Virginia, is a lot of fun for the little ones.

According to tradition, the cabbage fairy (no relation to the Cabbage Patch dolls), leaves money in the cabbage. With a whole lot of fanfare, a candle is lit and everyone goes into another room while the fairy does her work. Finally, Charlie says it's time and we all go check to see if the candle is out, signaling that money's in the pot and it's time to eat.

Charlie scoops out the cabbage, making sure a generous amount of change is also scooped out on the individual plates. The child is told "if" they eat all their cabbage they can keep the money. Whoever is brave enough to volunteer to do the dishes is allowed to keep all the money still left in the cabbage pot. (A great way to get them to do the dishes, I might add.)

This year we were truly celebrated out, and when Virginia asked if the cabbage fairy was coming, I responded, "Only if she's coming to your house and not mine!"

Being a good little trooper who loves tradition she put on quite a spread. As our granddaughter Amber filled her plate

Figure 8 - Tradition #1

(everything BUT cabbage) she said, "I'm so glad I have a real job now and don't need the money so I don't have to eat cabbage anymore!"

What a laugh that got from her Grandma. The little ones, however, were going back for seconds and I wondered who would wind up volunteering to do the dishes.

Traditions can be fun. I'm sure your household enjoyed a lot of family traditions during holidays; especially, when it came to your favorite holiday foods.

Tradition is one of those customs that are both good and bad. Jesus talked about tradition when speaking to a group of religious leaders. In Matthew 15 He accused the Pharisees of putting outward traditions above the true condition of the heart.

He said, "Thus you nullify the Word of God for the sake of your tradition. You hypocrites! Isaiah was right when he prophesied about you: 'These people honor Me with their lips, but their hearts are far from Me. They worship Me in vain; their teachings are but rules taught by men.'" (Matthew 15:7-8)

The Pharisees were worried about the proper way to wash one's hands. They were worried about what was going into the body, rather than what was coming out.

Later His disciples asked Him to explain His remarks to the Pharisees: "Are you so dull?" He asked. "Don't you see that nothing that enters a man from the outside can make him 'unclean?' For it doesn't go into his heart but into his stomach, and then out of his body.'" (Mark 7:18-19).

He went on: "What comes out of a man is what makes him 'unclean.' For from within, out of men's hearts, come evil thoughts, sexual immorality, theft, murder, adultery, greed, malice, deceit, lewdness, envy, slander, arrogance, and folly. All these evils come from inside and make a man 'unclean.'"

There are even some today who are relying on their religious traditions to get them to Heaven. "Forasmuch as ye know that ye were not redeemed with corruptible things, as silver and gold, from your vain conversation received by **tradition** from your fathers; But with the precious blood of Christ, as of a lamb without blemish and without spot" (I Peter 1:18-19).

God's Word does NOT change. If the Words of Jesus were true 2,000 years ago, they are just as true today. The Apostle Peter hit the nail on the head! The traditions of our fathers are vain. They will not help us obtain entrance into Heaven. Only salvation through the precious blood of Christ is necessary for our ticket into glory. Are your traditions good or bad when it comes to your eternal state? Happy New Year!

Figure 9 - Tradition #2

SCRIPTURES FOR MEDITATION

(Selah – think on these things)

MONDAY: *I will not allow the traditions of men to keep me from a true relationship with God.*

Scriptures: Judges 6:24-31; Matthew 7:21-23, 23:13-15; I Peter 1:18-19.

TUESDAY: *I will follow the examples of Godly persons.*

Scriptures: Joshua 1:1-7; 2 Kings 2:8-14; I Corinthians 11:1; Philippians 1:10, 3:17.

WEDNESDAY: *I will not be deceived by the ploys of the devil.*

Scriptures: Deuteronomy 11:16; I Kings 13:18-26; Proverbs 20:1; Matthew 24:35; 2 Timothy 3:12-17.

THURSDAY: *I will make the effort every day to listen to and obey God's voice.*

Scriptures: Exodus 18:19; Joshua 5:6; 2 Kings 18:12; 2 Chronicles 17:3-6; Jeremiah 43:1-7.

FRIDAY: *I will seek to be an example to others of a life lived for God.*

Scriptures: Psalms 101:2; Micah 6:8; I Timothy 4:12; I Thessalonians 4:14-17; Hebrews 11:32-40.

SATURDAY: *I will remember that what goes into my heart will affect my life.*

Scriptures: Numbers 32:6-9; Jeremiah 17:9; Matthew 5:8, 13:13-16; Hebrews 10:22.

Week 3
SIGNS OF THE TIMES

When it comes to controversy or confrontation, I'll be the first to admit that I'm a chicken. I would rather walk a mile out of my way than to face someone who is angry with me or who has a bone to pick. I guess that's why Charlie and I get along so well. We're both "lovers" not "fighters." When Charlie gets aggravated with me he's been known to retreat to his workshop or cut firewood. When I get upset I bang away at the keys on my computer. (I used to slam doors.)

This year Charlie and I are reading our bibles through again and it's always so refreshing to read the book of Genesis. In the first chapter God says, "Let there be lights in the firmament of the heaven to divide the day from the night; and let them be for signs, and for seasons, and for days, and years" (Gen. 1:14). The key thought here is "let them be for signs."

In contemplating some recent discussions involving horoscope columns, I decided to "come out of the closet" and officially go on record as opposing the propagation of forecasting one's future by this pagan method. While seemingly harmless, I am convinced the daily horoscopes that are plastered in the majority of newspapers are only a Pandora's Box, creating a springboard for other occult practices.

As a Christian, I accept the whole Bible as being the inerrant Word of God. It is impossible for me to discount or make light of the distinct warnings and prohibitions against prognosticators as set forth by God in the book of Deuteronomy (Deut. 18:9-12). In part this passage states: "There shall not be found among you any one . . . that useth divination, or an observer of times . . . ."

Jeremiah the prophet quoted God as saying, "I know the plans I have for you," declares the Lord, "plans to prosper you and not to harm you, plans to give you hope and a future" (Jer. 29:11 NIV). If you want to know who can foretell your future I can tell you in one word . . . GOD! He knows what is around the bend. He is the one who "knows the end from the beginning."

Figure 10 - Signs of the Times

There are some who would argue that reading your daily horoscope is just harmless fun. I strongly disagree. A close, personal friend of mine got so wrapped up in this "harmless" form of entertainment she eventually began going to fortune tellers to see what her future held. By the time she came to know Jesus Christ as her personal Savior she had spent several thousand dollars on books by every popular clairvoyant she could find. She celebrated her new-found faith with a bonfire. Edgar Cayce's books, along with all her other books of magic and witchcraft, went up in smoke. My friend began to lean on the true and living God, Who alone, holds the future in His hand!

In bible times we see a perfect example of burning the works of darkness in the book of Acts. "And many that believed came, and confessed, and shewed their deeds. Many of them also which used curious arts brought their books together, and burned them before all men: and they counted the price of them, and found it fifty thousand pieces of silver. So mightily grew the Word of God and prevailed" (Acts 19:18-20).

Witchcraft, channeling, horoscopes are all popular fads right now. Have you checked your TV Guide to see how many programs are dealing with witchcraft this season? You might be shocked. What started out as the, so-called harmless white witch, Samantha, in BEWITCHED, has now become full blown witchcraft, with teenage sisters in a weekly TV program, demonstrating the ancient arts of the underworld. Parents are sleeping, while their children are being enticed into the exciting and forbidden world of the occult.

Are there signs today? Pisces, Aquarius, etc.? What was God talking about in Genesis? Some farmers will tell you that the phase of the moon definitely has a bearing on when to plant certain crops. I believe there is only one sign we should be looking at today for our eternal welfare; the sign of our resurrected Savior.

Jesus said, "An evil and adulterous generation seeketh after a sign; and there shall no sign be given to it, but the sign of the prophet Jonas: For as Jonas was three days and three nights in the whale's belly; so shall the Son of man be three days and three nights in the heart of the earth" (Matthew 12:39-40).

There's your sign for the future . . . the living Christ. One who died and was buried and rose again on the third day. Look to that sign, friend, and you will never have to worry about your future.

SCRIPTURES FOR MEDITATION
(Selah – think on these things)

MONDAY: *I will repent for any seemingly innocent dealings that I may have had with any works of darkness such as: horoscopes, fortune tellers, Ouija boards, clairvoyants or any type of unbiblical prognosticators.*

Scriptures: Deuteronomy 18:9-11; I Samuel 28:7-18; Romans 13:12; Ephesians 5:11-12.

TUESDAY: *I will trust God for my future.*

Scriptures: Joshua 1:1-5; Isaiah 45:1-3, 58:11; Jeremiah 29:8-11; Lamentations 3:21-26.

WEDNESDAY: *I will walk in confidence each day with God.*

Scriptures: Joshua 22:5; Psalm 84:11; Proverbs 3:21-26, 28:1; Acts 4:29-31; Hebrews 13:5-6.

THURSDAY: *I will give God the glory for all the good that is accomplished in my life.*

Scriptures: 2 Samuel 1:19-27; Proverbs 16:18; Daniel 4:28-37; Jeremiah 9:23-24; Acts 12:21-24.

FRIDAY: *I will be firm in my belief that the Bible is the Word of God.*

Scriptures: Psalm 19:7-11, 119:160; John 17:17; Hebrews 4:12; Revelation 22:18-21.

SATURDAY: *I will be willing to stand up for truth.*

Scriptures: Exodus 32:26; Numbers 16:25-33; I Kings 18:21-39; Acts 7:54-60.

Week 4
ARE YOU UP TO THE CHALLENGE?

This past week I shared my testimony with some awesome ladies from my church, along with some equally awesome friends who joined us for Christian fellowship.

I don't share my salvation testimony very often, but sometimes it helps to take a step back in time and see where the Lord has brought you over the course of your life.

Since February is both my physical birth months as well as my spiritual birth month, it seemed appropriate to do as Isaiah said in his prophetic book. "Consider the rock you were cut out of. Think about the pit you were dug from" (Isa. 51:1).

In layman's language, "Don't forget your raising!"

Thanks to parents who accepted the Lord Jesus Christ as their Savior and to a Christian businessman who first talked to them about their lost condition, I had a dramatic conversion at a home Bible study.

Don Morsey believed that Jesus was Lord of his entire life, including his business life. I like to joke that God must have a sense of humor, because I believe He sprinkled black widow spiders all around my parent's house. Don, who owned a pest control company, came out to spray the little critters and before long, through his faithful witness to them; my dad and mom accepted Christ. Now, the real work began; how to get one rebellious kid (that would be me) under the sound of the Gospel.

I wasn't a likely candidate for the church. Most of the time church folks turn their noses up when they spot someone who rides with an outlaw biker gang (Hell's Angels); or someone who had been involved with activities too vile to publish in this book.

How thankful I am for the love and concern they showed to me, even though I fought them every step of the way. Most folks would have given up if they had been cussed at, reviled, and even had smoke blown in their faces.

Figure 11 - Riding with the Hell's Angels

Despite me, my folks loved me and every time they felt like giving up on me; Don would tell them to keep praying. And pray they did.

One night I finally gave in and went with them to a Bible study held in Don's home. I was forever changed! Somehow, through all my sin and rebellion God revealed Himself to me.

That night in February of 1957, I saw the face of Jesus shining through Don Morsey. If you ever see Jesus you will never be the same.

My passion has been to reflect my Savior, just as He was reflected in Don's face that night, long ago. If you ever really and truly get a glimpse of Him, you'll never want to go back to that old life of sin, sorrow and degradation.

Church is wonderful, but going to church doesn't turn you into a Christian, any more than going to McDonald's will turn you into a hamburger. Seeing Jesus? That will change you forever!

So . . . the adventure began. First, I shared Jesus with a Jewish girl, Frances Abraham. She became a believer in Yeshua (Jesus to you, Goyim). Then it was off to the Gentiles! (Goyim)

Along the way I had three wonderful daughters: Linda, Sandy, and Dotty. It wasn't long before I married Charlie and inherited his five awesome kids: Debi, David, John, Jeff, and Virginia. Soon we got another kid . . . Alan Raffield. Yikes! Our quiver was full.

When I last checked my calendar, I realized it has now been 60 years since I began my life in Christ and nearly 45 years since Charlie and I embarked on this journey called marriage.

I love my life. Yes, there have been ups and downs . . . when everything is even, it's called a flat line and you're dead. Every day is an adventure with Jesus.

In 1974 Charlie and I moved to Georgia. I thought nothing exciting would happen when we pulled up stakes and moved to this little town of 5,000 from the big city of Sacramento, California. Boy, was I ever wrong.

Since moving to Cochran, God has opened doors that I would have never dreamed possible. From starting a home bible class for local college students to traveling to countries like Mexico, Brazil, Ecuador, China, India, Israel and Costa Rica; I've learned there are no small places with God!

I've got a message burning in my heart that will change the world. I know. It's changed mine!

Yes, despite me, my folks loved me and every time they felt like giving up on me; Don would tell them to keep praying. They never gave up praying for me!

One night I finally gave in and went with them to a Bible study held in Don's home. I was forever changed! Somehow, through all my sin and rebellion God revealed Himself to me.

SCRIPTURES FOR MEDITATION

(Selah – think on these things)

MONDAY: *Today I rejoice that I am a child of God!*

Scriptures: Psalm 40:1-3; John 3:3-7, 20:30-31; I Corinthians 6:9-11; 2 Corinthians 5:17.

TUESDAY: *I refuse to go back to my old way of living.*

Scriptures: Proverbs 26:11; Luke 9:23-26; Luke 9:57-62; John 6:66-69; 2 Peter 2:20-22.

WEDNESDAY: *I will be on the lookout today for those who need Jesus.*

Scriptures: Proverbs 11:30; Daniel 12:2-3; John 1:45-46, 4:29, 42; Philemon 1:10-18.

THURSDAY: *I will not be discouraged if I don't see immediate results as I witness.*

Scriptures: Ecclesiastes 11:1-6; Isaiah 55:8-11; Matthew 13:18-23; Hebrews 11:32-40.

FRIDAY: *I will follow God's leading even if the job is small in the eyes of men.*

Scriptures: I Kings 17:8-15, I Kings 19:19; Zechariah 4:9-10; Matthew 10:42; Luke 16:10-11.

SATURDAY: *I will trust God to keep me faithful to Him when the going gets tough.*

Scriptures: Psalm 34:19; 2 Corinthians 11:23-28; 2 Timothy 3:12; Hebrews 11:24-27; James 1:2-4.

Week 5
ARE WE THERE YET?

That question was asked more than once as we made our way from California to Georgia back in 1974. Traveling with seven children in a Ford station wagon, during the oil embargo, was quite the experience.

We had two preschoolers (Dotty and Virginia); three middle school aged children (Sandy, Jeff, and Linda); and two teenagers (David and John). Fortunately, the oldest son, David had a driver's license and was able to help out with the driving. Our plan was to drive straight through without stopping in order to save on hotel bills.

I didn't know it snowed in Arizona. It was my turn to drive the late-night shift. Everyone was sleeping and I tried, almost in vain, to see the road through the snow-covered windshield. My wipers were straining to push the snow aside.

Soon I was creeping along the highway, following the tail lights of the vehicle in front of me. Everyone was sound asleep. Surely the snow would end soon. The car in front of me came to a stop. Horrified, I realized I was in someone's driveway. Are we there yet? Not hardly. "Honey, wake up," I said while shaking Charlie by the shoulder. "We're in someone's driveway." I didn't take the night shift again.

Missouri was beautiful. We had lots of stops along the way, mainly waiting for gas deliveries. Remember those days? On odd numbered days, you could purchase gas if your license plate ended on an odd number; likewise, with the even number plates on even numbered days.

After waiting three hours for a gas delivery, we finally filled the tank. The kids all piled in the car and we were off again. (This was in the days before seat belt requirements so the kids were always shifting around.) "Mom, stop! You forgot Linda." I thought they were kidding. Sure enough, we had gone ten miles before we realized we were shy one kid. (Yes, we went back and got her.)

Needless to say, our nerves were just about shot by this time. Are we there yet? Finally, we made our way to West Virginia. We had planned a stop to see Charlie's dear mother, Irma Ballengee. I had never met her and sure did want to meet the woman who had prayed for Charlie's salvation. In her words, "I carried that boy 'round my neck for 16 years.'" Her way of saying she was burdened for her wayward son and prayed daily for him.

Figure 12 - Are We There Yet?

While driving around the hairpin curves in the Appalachian Mountain Range, we were more than a little nervous when we came close to the edge and the drop off went hundreds of feet down into oblivion. Are we there yet? Hungry Mother Mountain just about did me in on that stretch of our journey. Whew!

After a few nights of visiting and sleeping in Grandma's little country home we set out for Georgia. We arrived in Warner Robins, GA at 2 a.m. and rented a few rooms in a seedy motel close to Robins AFB and adjacent to a railroad track. Around 4 a.m. the train went through our motel (not literally . . . but almost.) Are we there yet?

Soon we were settled into our 1885 farmhouse. Our kids got enrolled in school, eventually grew up and had children of their own; some even have grandchildren now. Are we there yet?

Life is really a journey. We never truly arrive, but only keep moving forward. With life come problems, challenges, rewards, and mistakes.

Sometimes we come to dead ends (Arizona); sometimes we make goofs (Missouri); sometimes we are in fearful situations (West Virginia); sometimes life has interruptions (trains in the middle of the night); sometimes there is lack (gas crisis); sometimes rewards (children, grandchildren, great-grandchildren), but we're still not there yet.

Every day is a new day on this journey. Only when we see our Savior face to face will we be able to say, "We're finally there!"

This past week I was privileged to lead a young man who has a terminal disease to Christ. As we sat in the office, I looked into his eyes and said, "You know you're in a place. This office is just a place. When we die we're going to another place; from one place to the next. This life is not our final destination. We're not there yet."

As I told him of the choice before him . . . the place of Heaven or the place of Hell, he made a decision to go to the right place. Tears streamed down both our faces as he gave his heart to the Lord. He's not there yet. Neither am I, but we are both headed in the right direction. Are you?

SCRIPTURES FOR MEDITATION

(Selah – think on these things)

MONDAY: *I will follow God wherever He leads!*

Scriptures: Genesis 12:1-4, 24:56-67; Ruth 1:15-18; Psalm 23:3, 139:1-10.

TUESDAY: *I know God is guiding my life because I have put my trust in Him.*

Scriptures: Ruth 2:12; Psalm 48:14, 56:3-4, 61:2; Proverbs 3:5-6; John 16:13.

WEDNESDAY: *I walk by faith and not by sight.*

Scriptures: Joshua 1:13-18; Mark 11:20-24; John 20:27-31; Hebrews 11:1-3, 11:8-10.

THURSDAY: *Although I cannot see Heaven I believe it is a real place.*

Scriptures: 2 Samuel 12:18-23; 2Kings 2:9-14; John 14:1-6; Acts 1:8-11; Revelation 4:1-5.

FRIDAY: *I will make my life count for eternity.*

Scriptures: Matthew 6:19-21, 25:21; Mark 12:41-44; Romans 14:10-12; I Corinthians 3:11-15.

SATURDAY: *I will remind myself that this life is short, but eternity is forever.*

Scriptures: Job 7:6-7; Psalm 90:1-10; Ecclesiastes 3:1-2; Isaiah 57:15; Daniel 7:9-13.

Week 6
ARE YOU DRIFTING?

My husband Charlie has several reading passions; two of them being Civil War history and World War II history. He was delighted when I went to a local consignment shop and obtained an entire set of World War II encyclopedias in mint condition for only twenty dollars.

The 24-volume set is prominently displayed in our living room bookcase. He enjoys perusing the black and white photos and information contained in each volume. I guess his penchant for this period in history goes back to his remembrance of that time period.

Always one to enjoy reading, Charlie told me he was reading *Hans Brinker* or, *The Silver Skates* when the announcement came over the airwaves that Pearl Harbor had been bombed. Much like, "Where were you on 9-11?" The World War II generation has the date of the Pearl Harbor bombing etched in their memories.

One of my personal favorite accounts of this time period is that of Louis Zamperini. I first heard Zamperini speaking at a Billy Graham crusade back in the '50s. Zamperini was a fascinating individual and lived until the ripe old age of 97.

Laura Hillenbrand, the #1 NYT bestselling author of *Seabiscuit*, wrote a book about Zamperini entitled *UNBROKEN*. (If you haven't read it, I heartily recommend this book for your library.) I wasn't able to put this book down. Her literary style, coupled with her knowledge of the facts of Zamperini's life, as well as her close friendship with him, makes for a great read.

What intrigued me most about Zamperini's story was the account of his amazing survival for 47 days on a raft in the Pacific Ocean. Zamperini, a former Olympic runner, had the stamina and the determination to beat the odds against him after he and several others were shot down in their B-24 while on a rescue mission.

Zamperini's plane, the Green Hornet, crashed in the ocean on May 27, 1943. Eight of the eleven aboard were killed. The raft the survivors were on had no supplies. They actually survived by eating small fish and by catching rain water. One of the men died on the 40th day.

Figure 13 - Are We There Yet?

While on the raft Zamperini made a bargain with God. (I've always heard there are no atheists in a foxhole!) Unfortunately, many who make deals with God have short memories and all bets are off when they survive and are back in the land of the living. Not so with Zamperini.

The raft drifted into enemy water. Zamperini and his companions had no idea where they were. It was only when the Japanese Navy captured them on the 47th day of their ordeal that they realized capture was infinitely worse than what they had been going through on the raft.

Words can't describe the torture Zamperini and his fellow airmen went through. For over two years Zamperini was physically tortured and subjected to psychological abuse. His success as an Olympic athlete seemed to be one of the main reasons a sadistic guard, whom the prisoners nicknamed *the Bird* had singled him out.

After completing the book, I couldn't quit thinking about the poignant fact of Zamperini drifting on that raft. I remembered a Scripture in the Bible that says, "We must pay the most careful attention, therefore, to what we have heard, so that we do not drift away" (Hebrews 2:1).

Are You Drifting?

This verse does not say anything about being careful not to sin, watch your language, don't wear revealing clothes, don't drink, do drugs, smoke or steal . . . no, it says we need to be careful that we don't "drift away."

Drifting doesn't take any thought or effort. Just relax . . . drift. How many people today are getting farther and farther away from God by drifting? They're not doing anything particularly wicked and sinful . . . they're just doing nothing but drifting.

We are instructed to pay careful attention to what we have heard. This word of caution by the writer of Hebrews is designed to prod us, to keep us from disaster.

Zamperini drifted into the enemy camp, where deprivation and torture awaited him. Just as he was singled out by Mutshurio Watanabe, aka *the Bird*, we too will be singled out by the enemy of our soul if we drift away from God! The Christian life must be an active life, especially when it comes to keeping our relationship with the Lord fresh and vital. Spending time with God each day is essential. Make it your goal today to stay close to the Lord!

SCRIPTURES FOR MEDITATION

(Selah – think on these things)

MONDAY: *I will determine to consider the Lord in all my decisions.*

Scriptures: Judges 6:18-20; I Samuel 15:13-29; Jonah 1:1-10; Matthew 19:16-22; Mark 8:34-37.

TUESDAY: *I will not be lazy in my spiritual walk with God.*

Scriptures: I Chronicles 28:8-9; Proverbs 4:20-23, 6:6-11; Isaiah 26:9; 2 Peter 1:5-11.

WEDNESDAY: *I will remember to keep my vows and promises to God.*

Scriptures: Numbers 30:2; Psalm 116:12-14; Ecclesiastes 5:4-5; Matthew 26:69-75; Mark 14:27-31.

THURSDAY: *I will not serve the Lord half-heartedly, but with all my might.*

Scriptures: Deuteronomy 6:5, 10:12; 2 Samuel 23: 8-12; Micah 6:8; Luke 10:25-27.

FRIDAY: *I will remember to sow good seed in order to reap a good harvest.*

Scriptures: Genesis 8:22; 2 Samuel 12:7-12; Matthew 25:14-30; Galatians 6:7-9; I Peter 5:1-4.

SATURDAY: *I will not live in the past, but I will go forward in God's strength.*

Scriptures: Genesis 19:17-26; Isaiah 43:18-19; Isaiah 54:1-8; John 8:1-11; I Corinthians 6:9-11.

Week 7
A JOURNEY'S END

The phone call was not totally unexpected, but it still shook me to my core. My spiritual father, Don Morsey had passed away. I didn't know what to say.

Every time Don called and every time I went to California to visit with him he would say the same thing, "I don't know why I'm still here. I'm ready to go to Heaven and see my precious Heavenly Father."

I knew. I counted on Don's prayers. He had been praying for me every day since 1956. He led my mom and dad to Jesus. Soon I was high on his prayer list and he continued to pray.

He prayed me into the Kingdom of God. He prayed me through the death of my first baby. He prayed for me when I went through a stormy, rocky marriage. He prayed for me when I went on mission trips to foreign countries, and when I went into prisons and jails to minister Christ to others.

Shortly after Don celebrated his 90th birthday, God called him home. His tired and weary body could no longer sustain him and he went to be with the Lord whom he had so faithfully served.

Along life's way we meet many special people. I've been privileged to know so many who have poured blessing into my life. They've been there for me when I was down and discouraged or when I was bouncing off the wall with joy.

I appreciate each and every one whom God has sent into my life, but none so much as Don Morsey. I guess the one who introduces us to the Lord, holds a really special spot in our hearts.

I couldn't make it to California for Don's memorial service, but I was asked to write a tribute to him that would be read by my brother, Doug Krieger. I considered that such a great honor and I hope the words I wrote will bless you and cause you to think about that special person who introduced you to Christ.

Don was a great "fisher of men." He was my role model for life and I pray that like Don, I will finish my race well.

A TRIBUTE TO DON MORSEY

There is no way I can adequately put into words my deep gratitude for what Don Morsey has meant to me through these many years.

In 1956 Don witnessed to my dad and step-mother, Bill and Margie Krieger. As a result of his faithful witness to them, they accepted Christ as their personal Savior and began attending a Bible study in Don's home.

As they grew in the Lord they began to tell Don and Jewel to pray for their children and especially for their rebellious daughter, Jerri.

My parents finally convinced me to go with them to Don's home at 2121 Carlotta Drive in Sacramento, CA. I had planned to go only one time, but that's all it took.

As Don began teaching the Bible that evening, I didn't see him, but instead I saw the Lord Jesus Christ. At that moment in February of 1957 I was gloriously saved. As I left their home that night, Jewel handed me a little book, entitled *Peace with God* by Billy Graham. I was forever changed.

During the next 57 years Don was a constant encouragement to me. A month rarely went by that he didn't call me two or three times just to let me know that he was praying for my husband and me. I appreciated those prayers. I counted on those prayers. And I will miss hearing his voice telling me that he was praying for us and was just calling to let us to know that he was praying . . . that he was so glad we were continuing to minister in the prisons.

Many times, he would say, "I just don't understand why I'm still here. I am ready to go see Jesus and Jewel."

I would always answer, "You're here because you're supposed to be praying for us, Papa Don."

A Journey's End

Figure 14 - A Tribute to Don Morsey

Today I know he is still talking to Jesus about us, but now, instead of talking to a Savior he has never seen, he is talking to Him face to face.

Don was 33 when I first met him. He was dynamic, energetic and tireless in his pursuit of the things of God. I can picture him like that again, telling everyone in Heaven that there is nothing more valuable than souls.

Thousands will be in Heaven because of Don. I am only one of them. Thank you, Papa Don, for seeing the value in my soul. I love you.

SCRIPTURES FOR MEDITATION

(Selah – think on these things)

MONDAY: *I will remember to pray for others.*

Scriptures: I Samuel 12:23; Matthew 7:7-8; Romans 1:9-11; Colossians 1:9-12; James 5:16.

TUESDAY: *I will have an open door in my home to share Christ with others.*

Scriptures: 2 Kings 4:8-17; Matthew 10:40-42, 25:34-40; Mark 6:7-11; I Corinthians 15:58.

WEDNESDAY: *I will not forget those who have made an impact on my life.*

Scriptures: Proverbs 1:8-9; Malachi 3:16; Romans 16:1-16; 2 Timothy 1:5-7; Hebrews 12:1-2.

THURSDAY: *I will not serve the Lord half-heartedly, but with all my might.*

Scriptures: Deuteronomy 6:5, 10:12; 2 Samuel 23: 8-12; Micah 6:8; Luke 10:25-27.

FRIDAY: *I will remember that faithfulness will be rewarded.*

Scriptures: Proverbs 20:6, 28:20; Matthew 25:21; I Corinthians 4:1-2, 15:58.

SATURDAY: *I will remember that God's work, done God's way, will remain forever.*

Scriptures: 2 Chronicles 15:7; Jeremiah 31:16; Matthew 6:19-21; I Corinthians 3:11-14; Revelation 21:3-7

Week 8
WHAT TRAIN?

At one time it was probably a bustling place of business. The old bank, with an addition tacked on the side, was now converted in to a residence. The owners had done everything they could to make it a beautiful home. The biggest problem in marketing their home, I explained to them, was the close proximity of the house to the railroad tracks.

Undaunted, I listed the home, assuring the owners I would do everything within my power as a real estate professional, to procure a sale for them. Inwardly I groaned, wondering how I could convince anyone to live that close to a railroad track!

As a real estate agent, I tried to point out all the positive features of a piece of property, while discreetly downplaying the negatives. After all, a railroad track only forty feet from the front door, doesn't exactly qualify a house to be the featured "Home of the Month."

Later, while showing the house to a prospective buyer, I was asked the dreaded question regarding the frequency of trains coming by the house. Taking a deep breath, I answered cheerfully, "Oh, not often, maybe once or twice a day."

Figure 15 - What Train?

Just then we both turned. Coming our way was a roaring train; without any need to do so we both automatically jumped back, startled by the train's warning whistle. For several minutes, although it seemed like an eternity to me, we watched as the huge freight train went speeding by (as did my sale!).

As a country dweller now for nearly forty-three years I can't imagine how anyone can live close to a railroad track, an airport, or for that matter any noisy industrial complex. (As a side note, I finally managed to sell that particular house to another buyer. Whew!)

Some years back, Charlie and I were invited to share our testimonies at a Methodist church in Forest Park, Georgia. One of the parishioners was kind enough to invite us to spend the night in his lovely home. There was little sleep for the two visitors from rural Georgia! It seemed as though every thirty seconds or so a plane was going to land in our bedroom. The next day two, bleary-eyed people shared with the congregation that Jesus loved them. Yawn! (I wanna go home.)

It's all in what you get used to.

Friend, Patti Molzen, moved to Norcross, Georgia. Before her move to the big city she lived near the railroad tracks in our town. No problem according to Patti, "You just get used to the noise." So, what if you can't hear the TV for a few minutes or carry on a conversation; after a while you don't even hear the pesky train. You become CONDITIONED.

Today we're living in a society where nearly everyone is CONDITIONED! Think about it. Was it only eighty or so years ago that the world was shocked when Rhett Butler told the naughty Scarlett O'Hara that he frankly didn't give a _ _ _ _? (Don't blush folks . . . you hear more than that on the nightly news!) Imagine . . . the remake of *Gone With The Wind* was given a "G" rating!

Without trying to sound too much like a Puritan, I'm afraid I've also become much too CONDITIONED. What once shocked me, doesn't seem to have the same effect anymore. (Although I still turn Cosmopolitan magazine over every time I get the chance to do so, while waiting in line at a grocery store.)

Today, Playboy is considered mild and shows like the now defunct Jerry Springer show is standard afternoon fare for bored housewives and teeny boppers alike. Oprah Winfrey espouses a mix of Christianity and New Age philosophy, as loyal, adoring fans drink in her rhetoric as though it were solid Gospel preaching. (OOPS! Did I get your sacred cow that time?) Then there are those who would rather see Bruce Willis (a man who claims Biblical Christianity is on its way out), in

"Armageddon," than read the prophetic account of the end times from the Bible; which, in my opinion and that of a few million other people, is the only Book that gives the original and true scoop on what's really going to happen in the end!

For a homework assignment I once gave my Jr. High Sunday School class the task of writing down how many curse words they heard in an evening of watching television; the result? There were so many curse words the class, as a whole, quit counting. Are you shocked? Or are you saying, "So what?"

Hey! Wake up fellow Christians. Let's admit we've become CONDITIONED! We no longer hear the roar of the train anymore. We're so bogged down with the philosophies and language of the world that nothing seems to offend us like it once did. We need to shake off our lethargy, repent of our compromising, admit we are desensitized and realize the train is not only coming down the track . . . it's headed our way!

Since many of you have now joined the ranks of the computer literate, let me remind you . . . GARBAGE IN . . . GARBAGE OUT! There is no way that we have not been affected, to some degree, with the sleaze of this world. My appeal to you is that we all, voluntarily, turn off the tube. Let's refuse to let our minds become a garbage dump. Post a "No Dumping" sign where it counts. Ask the Lord to once again let us become sensitive to the promptings of the Holy Spirit. Let's become a people of HOLINESS. Let's raise a standard in our homes. It's not too late. I can hear the train coming, but there's still time!

"For the grace of God that brings salvation has appeared to all men. It teaches us to say 'No' to ungodliness and worldly passions, and to live self-controlled, upright and godly lives in this present age, while we wait for the blessed hope—the glorious appearing of our great God and Savior, Jesus Christ" (Titus 2:11-12).

SCRIPTURES FOR MEDITATION
(Selah – think on these things)

MONDAY: *I will choose a life of separation.*

Scriptures: Judges 13:2-7; Ezra 9:1-3; Psalm 1:1-3; Jeremiah 10:2; Romans 12:1-2; 2 Corinthians 6:14-18.

TUESDAY: *I know God is a Holy God and delights in Holiness.*

Scriptures: Exodus 15:11; Leviticus 20:26; Isaiah 6:1-3; Zechariah 14:20-21; Hebrews 12:14.

WEDNESDAY: *I will not point my finger at others, but will extend grace.*

Scriptures: Genesis 33:1-11; 2 Samuel 9:1-13, 12:1-7; Romans 14:1-4; Philemon 1:10-18.

THURSDAY: *I will remember to guard my heart.*

Scriptures: Joshua 24:15; Psalm 101:3, 119:37; Proverbs 4:23; Luke 6:45; Acts 13:22.

FRIDAY: *I will determine to lift up a standard in my home and community.*

Scriptures: Genesis 18:19; Exodus 17:10-12; Isaiah 13:2, 49:22, 59:19, 62:10.

SATURDAY: *I will remember that nothing is impossible with God.*

Scriptures: Exodus 14:13-16; Isaiah 43:19; Mark 9:23; Luke 1:26-35; Revelation 11:3-12.

Week 9
FINDING THE RAINBOW

Just a teenager, sixteen-year-old Patrick was carried off by a band of Irish raiders and taken as a slave to Ireland. He was sold to a tribal chieftain named Milchu. For six years he worked as a herdsman, all the while praying for deliverance. The kidnapping happened around the year 405 AD.

As Providence would have it, Patrick acquired a perfect knowledge of the Celtic tongue and since his master was a Druid high priest, he also became knowledgeable with all the ins and outs of the satanic religion of Druidism.

Later writings show that Patrick's faith grew in captivity. He felt that he was in constant communication with God. One day he heard a voice telling him that he would soon go home on a ship. He took this as a green light and fled his master, traveling on foot to port two hundred miles away.

After returning home he became active in the Catholic Church. Legend has it that Patrick had a vision about a man coming to him from Ireland. The man's name was Victoricus and he was carrying many letters. Victoricus handed Patrick a letter entitled, *The Voice of the Irish*. As Patrick began reading he imagined that he heard the voice of the Irish calling out to him to come to Ireland and walk among them.

Through Patrick's efforts as a messenger of the Gospel, many turned from the hopeless belief of paganism and gave their hearts to Christ as the only Savior and God. His period of slavery, which seemed to be a tragedy at the time, turned out to be a good thing in the long-range plan of God.

As we celebrate St. Patrick's Day every March 17th we need to remember the story of this brave young man and be inspired to reach out and help others.

So many times, we look at the problems we're going through and can't imagine that anything good can result from them. Yet, if we believe the Scriptures we can take heart. In the Old Testament, we read that God makes everything beautiful in His time (Ecclesiastes 3:11); and in the New Testament we are reminded that "all things work together for good to them that love God and are called according to His purpose" (Romans 8:28).

Figure 16 - Finding the Rainbow

Charlie and I recently watched as Lee Ezell shared her testimony on Sky Angel. She had come from an abusive home but just prior to graduation she accepted Christ as her Savior. Now, everything should be wonderful; right? Wrong. Bad things do happen to good people, whether we want to admit it or not.

Just out of high school Lee got her first job. A traveling salesman talked her into going out with him. On that first date he raped her and then disappeared out of her life. At first, she couldn't believe she was pregnant, but soon everyone knew. As a Christian, abortion was not a consideration. She read Psalm 139 and saw that life, even the life inside her, was created by God and ordained by him.

Lee, like Moses' mother, gave the child up in a closed adoption proceeding. Twenty years later she received a phone call. "My name is Julie. You don't know me, but I'm your daughter. I prayed I would find you so I could tell you about Jesus and how to get to Heaven."

The reunion was more than great! The two appeared on several TV talk shows. Their story touched countless lives and who knows how many babies were saved in the process. Julie's husband told her mom that he was glad she didn't administer the death penalty to Julie because of her father's sin. (Lee has written a book entitled, *The Missing Piece*, her experience - available on Amazon.com)

Today you may be in a tough spot in life. It might not be as bad as Patrick's or Lee's situations, but nonetheless you are wondering how in the world anything good can come of it. Put your hand in the Lord's hand and let Him walk you through this trial. You have God's very own promise that this will work out for good. In the end you'll find your rainbow.

SCRIPTURES FOR MEDITATION

(Selah – think on these things)

MONDAY: *I will be thankful for the rainbows that follow the storms in my life.*

Scriptures: Genesis 9:12-17, 50:18-21; 2 Kings 1:4-7; Romans 8:28-31; Revelation 1:9-18.

TUESDAY: *I am confident that God is in control even when things look bleak.*

Scriptures: Exodus 14:13-16; 2 Samuel 22:31; Job 23:10; Psalm 23:4-5, 56:3, 139:12.

WEDNESDAY: *I will go the extra mile to help those in need.*

Scriptures: Isaiah 58:5-8; Luke 10:25-37; Acts 16:9; Ephesians 4:28; 2 Timothy 1:16-18; James 1:27.

THURSDAY: *I will not give up on people because God never gave up on me.*

Scriptures: 2 Kings 5:1-16; Psalms 107:9-15; John 4:15-19, 8:2-11; I Timothy 1:12-15.

FRIDAY: *I believe the Lord is with me in every trial that I experience.*

Scriptures: Genesis 31:38-42; Psalms 27:1-6; Daniel 3:22-25, 6:16-22; Romans 8:37-39.

SATURDAY: *I will use my experiences to help others.*

Scriptures: I Samuel 22:1-2; John 4:25-29; Acts 16:26-34, 28:1-9; 2 Corinthians 1:1-10.

Week 10
DRESSED FOR THE OCCASION

One of my girlfriends has the unique benefit of being able to fly anywhere in the world by using a "buddy pass." Since her husband works for a major airline their family is able to purchase tickets at an incredibly reduced rate. Recently, thanks to her "buddy pass," she had a fabulous vacation in Cancun.

She shared her latest experience with those of us who had joined her for lunch at a local restaurant. It seems the airline her husband works for has a very strict dress code requirement for the employees and their families.

She had no idea that her newly purchased shoes would be unacceptable attire because they had no backs on them. Trying to convince the flight attendant of the absurdity of the requirement was useless. Since she was informed about the rule an hour before departure she began to search for a store in the terminal that might sell shoes.

It was no use! Starbucks yes . . . Payless Shoes no! That's when Dee began to size up the shoe sizes of fellow passengers. "Hmmm," she thought, "that lady looks like she might be wearing my size."

She was desperate. Either she had the right shoes or she would be kissing her husband and two daughters good-by.

"Ma'am," she implored, "what size shoe do you wear?"

Dee began to share her predicament with the woman. All I have to say about this encounter is that Dee is a pretty good salesperson. Within minutes the two strangers had exchanged shoes and Dee was happily on her way to Cancun with her family. After the all-clear sign was given in the cabin, Dee made her way to seat 27A and gave the lady back her shoes.

As we sat laughing about the incident; the other friend shared how her son had a similar problem. He also had a buddy pass and was on his way to meet his wife in Florida with his two small daughters. He had no idea he couldn't wear shorts on the flight.

Figure 17 - Dressed for the Occasion

Taking his little girls by the hand he raced from store to store through the terminal looking for a place to buy a pair of pants. As departure time was upon him he begged the airline attendant to let him on the plane, explaining that he didn't know the rules.

Finally, in desperation he pleaded with them saying he was a pastor and they could trust him to make sure it would never happen again. Apparently, they took pity on the young man with the two little blonde-headed girls and allowed him on the plane.

Since I didn't have a "buddy pass" story to share I thought I would share the story in the Bible that tells about a man who came to a wedding without a proper wedding garment.

Back in the Bible days guests were required to wear special attire to get into a wedding party. The interesting part of the story is that everyone was given an invitation.

Many people gave excuses why they couldn't come to the wedding. One had to tend to his farm, another had his business, and another had family responsibilities. Of those who did come, one came to the door without a proper wedding garment.

When questioned, the guest was speechless. He couldn't think of a single good reason for his unpreparedness. "Then the king said to the servants, 'Bind him hand and foot, and take him away, and cast him into outer darkness; there shall be weeping and gnashing of teeth.'" (Matthew 22:13)

When we arrive at the judgment we won't be able to talk someone into exchanging their wedding garment, neither will we be able to convince God that we're a good person (pastor or not). Each of us must prepare beforehand for our departure from this earth.

Even though we had a good laugh over Dee's and the pastor's near misses on the airplanes, no one except God, will be laughing on the Day of Judgment.

"He who sits in the heavens shall laugh, the Lord scoffs at them. Then He will speak to them in His anger and terrify them in his fury . . . Do homage to the Son, that He not become angry, and you perish in the way" (Psalm 2).

SCRIPTURES FOR MEDITATION

(Selah – think on these things)

MONDAY: *I am grateful that I am clothed with the righteousness of Christ.*

Scriptures: Isaiah 64:6; Jeremiah 23:1-6; Zechariah 3:1-5; Matthew 5:20; I Corinthians 1:29-31.

TUESDAY: *I am grateful that Jesus paid the price for my ticket to Heaven.*

Scriptures: Isaiah 6:1-7; John 12:23-27, 14:1-6, 19:30; Hebrews 10:14-22.

WEDNESDAY: *Today I will willingly share the Good News of the Gospel.*

Scriptures: Matthew 4:17-22; John 4:28-30; Acts 20:18-24; Romans 10:13-17; 2 Peter 3:9.

THURSDAY: *I will remember that standing before God is not a laughing matter.*

Scriptures: Psalm 2:1-4; Daniel 7:9-10, 12:1-3; Matthew 22:10-13; Revelation 20:11-15.

FRIDAY: *I will remember that choices determine destiny.*

Scriptures: Genesis 13:7-13; Deuteronomy 30:15-20; I Kings 18:21; John 3:16; John 5:24.

SATURDAY: *I will boldly declare to the world that Jesus is Lord.*

Scriptures: Jeremiah 20:9; Matthew 28:18-20; Acts 1:6-8, 4:13-31; Philippians 1:20.

Week 11
NEEDLE IN A HAYSTACK

Sandy sounded pretty frantic at the other end of the line. "Mom, you really have to pray. I've lost my car key and it's the only one I have." Assuming it was in her house somewhere I wasn't too concerned. Then she dropped the bomb! She had been hunting arrowheads on a 400-acre tract of land out in the country! Groan.

Several of our grandchildren are also avid arrowhead hunters. Eli, our grandson, who was nine-years-old at the time, seemed to find more arrowheads than anyone else in the family. Just as I hung up the phone, Eli and his brother Zach walked into my kitchen. They had been fishing with their dad, grandpa, and several uncles. They were hungry and looking for some homemade soup.

I immediately conscripted Eli for the job of helping his Aunt Sandy. We drove away from the house leaving everyone to fend for themselves until we returned. "We'll be back," I said cheerily, "just as soon as we find Sandy's key."

Inwardly I just knew, that with God's help, and the fact that Eli was built pretty close to the ground, we would find Sandy's missing key.

On the way out to the country, I encouraged Eli with promises from God's Word about finding lost things. I had recently found a necklace that had been missing for seven years, so this had truly bolstered my confidence in our amazing God.

When we reached our destination, I looked at the immensity of the task. There, stretched out before us, were acres and acres of freshly plowed ground. Sandy informed us that she had been hunting for several hours and hadn't been paying any attention to where she had been.

Undaunted at the task before us I said, "Let's pray!" We held hands, claiming the Scripture that says, "If two of you agree as touching anything they ask, it shall be done for them." And so, off we went, heads down, eyes scanning the ground as we all tramped over the Georgia dirt.

"Mom," lamented Sandy with tears brimming in her eyes, "it will be a miracle if we find that key." I told her it sure would be, and after a few more reassuring words we continued to search. God's Word is true no matter how things look! Eli agreed and we continued walking.

Calling in more troops, Sandy went to meet her daughters, who were also coming to help. The search continued in earnest. After another 45 minutes, I heard a joyful shout. Sandy, who was about a thousand feet from us near a grove of trees, yelled out, "I found it! I found it!" Needless to say, when we caught up with her, we all stopped to pray and thank the Lord. As Eli and I drove back to my house to get some of that good homemade soup, we rejoiced in what God had done for us.

Figure 18 - Needle in a Haystack

You know, God sees where we are too. You may not realize this if you're a lost person, but God has you in His sights. One little key, somewhere on 400 acres, but God knew the exact location, just like He knows where you are. The lost key could not fulfill its purpose out in that field. It was only when Sandy placed it in her car's ignition that it did what it was created to do.

Dear one, you were created for something better than lying in the dirt of this world; fulfill your destiny. "The Son of man has come to seek and to save those who are lost" (Luke 19:10).

SCRIPTURES FOR MEDITATION

(Selah – think on these things)

MONDAY: *I'm so glad the Lord knows where I am at every moment of every day.*

Scriptures: 2 Chronicles 16:9; Psalm 11:4, 34:15; Proverbs 15:3; Jeremiah 23:24; Zechariah 4:10.

TUESDAY: *I believe in the power of prayer.*

Scriptures: Exodus 3:7; Numbers 20:16; I Samuel 1:10-17; Matthew 18:19; Luke 18:1-8.

WEDNESDAY: *I will remember there is nothing too hard for God.*

Scriptures: Genesis 15:17-21; Joshua 10:12-14; Luke 1:31-37; John 9:1-7, 11:40-44.

THURSDAY: *I will not be a quitter.*

Scriptures: Joshua 10:15-25; Ecclesiastes 9:10-11; I Corinthians 9:24; 2 Timothy 4:7-8.

FRIDAY: *I will give God the glory for all my answered prayers.*

Scriptures: I Samuel 1:26-28; 2 Kings 6:17; Psalm 40:1-3, 107:1-2, 126:1-3.

SATURDAY: *I will remember God has a plan for my life.*

Scriptures: Psalm 139:12-16; Isaiah 45:1-6; Jeremiah 1:4-10; John 1:48-50; Acts 9:10-16, 26:15-19.

Figure 19 - The Road Less Traveled

Week 12
ALL ROADS LEAD TO WHERE?

Many years ago we used to take our grandchildren to church with us. At that time, we traveled about 25 miles one way, which gave us a lot of time to listen to Christian programming on our radio, (*Unshackled* was our favorite.) or have great discussions about spiritual things and life in general.

When our granddaughter, Amber, was a thirteen-year-old the discussions ranged from computers to poetry, to life in general. On one particular drive home, when Amber had been unusually talkative she grinned and said, "I'm just rambling on and on, aren't I Grandma?"

I laughed. I loved the lively discussions we always had on our trips home from youth meetings. "No," I said, trying to encourage her, "I enjoy knowing what's going on in your life."

Then, without prompting, she quoted Robert Frost's poem, "The Road Not Taken." Shirley Smith, her literature teacher, had assigned the poem by one of America's favorite poets, to the students in Amber's eighth grade class, for memorization.

I was struck with the similarity of the last verse, where it appears that M. Scott Peck, writer of the popular, *The Road Less Traveled* has modified the phrase ". . . I took the one less traveled by . . ." for the title to his book.

Figure 20 - All Roads Lead to Where?

Peck, at one time a practicing psychotherapist, wrote the book in the late seventies, approaching religion from a scientific position. He leads the reader to conclude there are multiple paths of approaching the same spot, allowing one to look at "so-called" spiritual truths without fear. With Peck emphasizing that paradox is key to spiritual understanding, and that questioning "everything" is a must, the reader is ultimately directed to the conclusion that any road will do.

In Frost's poem he ends with: "Somewhere ages and ages hence: Two roads diverged in a wood, and I, I took the one less traveled by, and that has made all the difference."

What a great springboard for our discussion! "Amber," I asked, "Do you see what the poet is saying? The road he chose, in ages to come, will make all the difference?"

We rode in silence for a while.

Amber, who had always been a big fan of Bunyan's classic, *Pilgrims Progress*, could easily see the parallel. It *does* make a difference which road you take in life. Even as little Christian, the book's hero, had to follow the hard road at times, his choices affected his destiny. The allegory pointed out that, the right road was sometimes the hard one, and definitely *the road less traveled*. In the end however, Christian made it to the Celestial City, and all the hardships on the narrow road were worth the sacrifices he made.

Today, whether you're young or old, you're faced with choices . . . roads, if you please. The philosophers, mystics, prognosticators and even the religious may tell you to find peace in your "inner self" . . . that all roads are okay. By doing this you may even wind up like the man in the Judean wilderness. When asked by someone why he was wandering around aimlessly, he answered, "I'm looking for myself."

Friend, there is a road less traveled. It's Jesus. Either He was the biggest liar and fake that ever existed, deceiving millions through the centuries, or what He said was truth. If you say you believe the Bible, what do you do with His claim, "I am the WAY, the truth and the life?"

If He *is* the WAY, as he claimed to be, then what? Can just any path do? In your quest for self-realization and fulfillment, what have you done with Him? In your search for happiness you've acquired a lot of "things," but are you on the right road? Will your ultimate end be that Celestial City Bunyan wrote about? For those of you who have a following, whether it be your family . . . your friends . . . your business associates .

. . students under your charge . . . where are you leading them? We all have influence. Are we headed in the right direction with that influence?

If Jesus Christ is really the WAY . . . if He is not a liar . . . then what? "Somewhere ages and ages hence . . . I took the one less traveled by, and that has made all the difference."

SCRIPTURES FOR MEDITATION
(Selah – think on these things)

MONDAY: *I will stay on the straight and narrow way for it leads to life.*

Scriptures: Numbers 22:21-35; Proverbs 2:10-20, 4:18; Isaiah 35:8-10; Matthew 7:13-14.

TUESDAY: *I will not be drawn aside with words of flattery and deceit.*

Scriptures: Psalm 1:1-2, 12:1-4; Proverbs 7:21, 12:22-24; Isaiah 29:13; Romans 16:18.

WEDNESDAY: *I will continue to teach my children and grandchildren the ways of the Lord.*

Scriptures: Genesis 18:19; Deuteronomy 4:9-14, 6:4-7, 11:19; 2 Timothy 1:5.

THURSDAY: *I will be an example to my children and grandchildren.*

Scriptures: 2 Chronicles 34:1-2; Proverbs 23: 19-26; I Timothy 1:7-20, 4:12.

FRIDAY: *I will not be taken in by today's philosophies that all roads lead to God.*

Scriptures: I Samuel 12:23; Psalm 73:17-18; Proverbs 14:12-15; Jeremiah 9:23-24; John 14:6.

SATURDAY: *I will keep my eyes upon the goal.*

Scriptures: Matthew 6:33; 2 Corinthians 4:18; Philippians 3:13-14; Hebrews 11:16; Revelation 1:7.

Week 13
VISION PROBLEMS

One summer a few years ago our church held a 3-Day Vacation Bible School (VBS) in a local housing project area. On the second day, I had an innovative idea to paint my fingernails the colors of the Wordless book. The technician at the nail shop was a little taken aback when I asked him if he could paint my fingernails different colors but, nonetheless, he fulfilled my request.

The paint job had the desired result. Little children were fascinated by the bright and cheery colors as they registered for the three-day VBS event. I, in turn, was delighted to share the Gospel story using the colors.

For those not familiar with this teaching tool, the colors stand for various truths contained in the Bible. Black stands for sin; Red for the blood of Christ; White for the clean heart the Lord gives when we receive Him as our personal Lord and Savior; Gold for the streets of gold in our heavenly, eternal home; and Green for the growth involved in the Christian life through reading our bibles and praying.

Since I've always had a love for telling stories, I had a great time telling the most important story in the world over and over again during the week of VBS and for the following two months. Many people were curious about the reasoning behind my multi-colored nails, and would ask, "What . . . or . . . Why?"

During this time, I went to a correctional facility to eat lunch with a friend. One of the employees, also at the luncheon, was wondering why I had been allowed into the facility because it appeared to him that I was wearing gang colors on my nails. Since there was a group of employees present; he didn't voice his concern (I found out this tidbit of information later.). However, I did notice he would glance at my fingernails from time to time.

Finally, I decided to meet his curious looks head on and asked him if he had been wondering about the color of my nails. When he said yes, I proceeded to share the story with him.

He got quite a laugh out of that and told me he was legally color blind. To him the colors looked black and white, which I learned were gang colors. Subsequently, he shared with all of us about his color blindness.

When he turned to go back to work I reminded him, with my gold painted index fingernail, there was only one way to Heaven . . . through Jesus Christ.

He said, "I have no idea what gold looks like."

Figure 21 – The Colors Tell the Story

Those of us who are able to see color can't fathom a world without it. Seeing, yet not seeing. Without color there is no depth, no defining lines. This became obvious when we went to wash our hands. For the first time this man noticed a soap dispenser in the small kitchenette at the facility. Since the soap dispenser and the wall were the same color, he had never noticed it, but when he saw us using it he realized it was there.

Color blindness, according to the experts, may be a hereditary condition or caused by a disease of the optic nerve or retina. Inherited color blindness is the most common, affecting both eyes, and does not worsen over time.

This type of color blindness is found in about 8% of males and 0.4% of females. These color problems are linked to the X chromosome and are almost always passed from a mother to her son. Complete color blindness is very rare, yet this dear man apparently had an extreme condition.

Nothing can be done to correct this man's condition, but if a cure were ever developed I believe he would be first in line.

Do you remember when you were blind? Not color blind, but spiritually blind. The condition was not your fault. You were born blind, because your parents, your grandparents and your entire family line had this spiritual disease and then passed it down to you

Suppose one day you are told there is a cure for your blindness and there is no cost for the cure! You are told the cost has been absorbed by the company who produced the cure. Would you take it? I think so.

I have even better news. Salvation is free for all, through the precious blood, shed by Jesus Christ on the cross. If you will only accept this cure for sin you can sing with millions who have taken the cure, "Once I was blind, but now I can see." Amazing race!

SCRIPTURES FOR MEDITATION
(Selah – think on these things)

MONDAY: *I will remember that children are valuable in God's sight.*

Scriptures: Deuteronomy 6:6-7; I Samuel 2:18-21, 3:1-16; Mark 10:14.

TUESDAY: *I will remember that the Gospel is simple so that all can understand.*

Scriptures: Matthew 11:25-26; Luke 10:20-21; John 3:16, 5:24; Acts 2:39; 2 Timothy 1:5.

WEDNESDAY: *I will remember that spiritual blindness is the condition of all lost persons.*

Scriptures: Psalm 146:8; Isaiah 29:18, 42:6-7; Matthew 15:14, 23:24-26.

THURSDAY: *I will share the Good News of the Gospel so the spiritually blind will see!*

Just Jerri

Scriptures: 2 Kings 6:17; Isaiah 61:1-3; Luke 24:29-32; John 9:1-25; Acts 9:10-18, 26:13-20.

FRIDAY: *I will remember that salvation is a free and is available to all who will receive.*

Scriptures: I Chronicles 16:23-25; Psalm 25:5, 40:16, 132:16; Isaiah 25:9; Ephesians 2:8-9.

SATURDAY: *I will never forget that I was once lost and on my way to Hell.*

Scriptures: Psalm 34:6, 40:1-3; Isaiah 45:22, 51:1; I Corinthians 6:9-11; 2 Corinthians 5:17.

Week 14
FOREVER STAMP

In March 1860, William H. Russell, an American transportation pioneer, advertised in newspapers as follows: "Wanted: Young, skinny, wiry fellows not over 18. Must be expert pony riders willing to risk death daily. Orphans preferred."

Now, of course I don't remember the Pony Express days, but I am old enough to remember when sending a letter would cost three cents, and if you wanted to save a little, you could use a penny postcard to address your sentiments to friends and relatives. On January 26, 2014 postage rates were raised to 49 cents. I told Charlie that if our health holds out and the Lord doesn't come we'll see a dollar stamp on letters. No telling what it will cost to send a letter by the year 2020.

Figure 22 - Forever Stamp

You may remember that in March of 2007, the first Forever Stamp went on sale for 41 cents. Then Postmaster General and Chief Executive Officer John E. Potter, when presenting the stamp at the National Postal forum was quoted as saying: "Who said nothing lasts forever? The stamp features the Liberty Bell image and the word *forever*. It will be good for mailing one-ounce First-Class letters anytime in the future, regardless of price changes." Wish I had bought several hundred of those stamps. I could have saved $16!

If you're wondering why the postal department did this, they have two reasons. First, by doing this, they don't have to make one, two, and three cent stamps in large quantities any more, as these stamps now cost as much or more to make than their face value. Secondly, those purchasing the Forever Stamp when it was on sale for a paltry 0.39 allowed the USPS to use that money immediately; while on the other hand, the purchaser might not use those stamps for a very long time. They may even get lost and never used. This allows the postal service to maximize the use of funds generated by the sale of those stamps.

To put it bluntly, it's a sales gimmick. There ain't no free lunch, folks. The only things that are forever are those things that God has put into motion.

To begin with, God is forever and eternally existent. God has no beginning and no end (Deut. 33:27). He has always been and will always be. Our finite minds may have trouble comprehending an infinite God, but nonetheless He is who He says He is.

God's Word is forever. Jesus said, Heaven and Earth will pass away but His Word will abide forever (Matt. 24:35). The psalmist put it this way, "Forever, O Lord, thy Word is settled in Heaven" (Psalm 89:10).

Your soul lasts forever. Paul states emphatically that the Christian shall EVER be with the Lord (I Thessalonians 4:14-18). For the soul without Christ, the Bible states that those who are without Christ, when they depart this life, are tormented day and night, forever and ever (Revelation 20:10).

Before the use of adhesive paper stamps, letters were hand stamped or postmarked with ink. Postmarks were the invention of Henry Bishop and were at first called "Bishop Mark" after the inventor. Bishop Marks were first used in 1661 at the London General Post Office. They marked the day and month the letter was mailed.

When a person receives the Lord Jesus Christ as Savior his heart is personally stamped by God. The mark is not visible to man, but it's a mark that is seen by God, the angels and the demons. In the Bible a story is told about those who were marked by God with a visible sign.

Then the LORD called to the man clothed in linen, the one who had the writing kit at his side, and said to him, "Go throughout the city of Jerusalem and put a mark on the foreheads of those who grieve and lament over all the detestable things that are done in it." As I listened, he said to the others, "Follow him through the city and kill, without showing pity or compassion. Slaughter old men, young men and maidens, women and children, but do not touch anyone who has the mark. Begin at my sanctuary." So, they began with the elders who were in front of the temple (Ezekiel 9:4-6).

I'm so glad that I have my Forever Stamp in place. Jesus is the Shepherd and Bishop of my soul (I Peter 2:25). I have His mark. The day and month the mark was placed on my heart was the last Thursday in February 1957. Are you marked or stamped by God?

SCRIPTURES FOR MEDITATION

(Selah – think on these things)

MONDAY: *I will be focused on the brevity of life compared to the eternity to follow.*

Scriptures: Job 7:6; Psalm 48:14, 90:12; Ecclesiastes 3:1-2, 21; Luke 16:19-31; Revelation 22:20.

TUESDAY: *I will remember that God has always been and will always be.*

Scriptures: Exodus 3:13-14; Psalm 90, 93:2; Isaiah 57:15; Daniel 7:9-14; Revelation 1:8.

WEDNESDAY: *I will remember that the Word of God is everlasting.*

Scriptures: I Samuel 3:19; Psalm 19:7; Isaiah 40:6-8; Matthew 24:35; I Peter 1:23-25.

THURSDAY: *I will remember that I am a carrier of the Word of God.*

Scriptures: Jeremiah 1:4-9, 20:9; Habakkuk 2:2; Luke 10:1-2; Romans 10:13-17.

FRIDAY: *I will not be discouraged if people do not receive the message of the Gospel.*

Scriptures: Joshua 1:5-9; Jeremiah 1:8; Ezekiel 3: 16-21; Matthew 26:56; 2 Timothy 4:10-17.

SATURDAY: *I will remember that one day even the smallest act of kindness will be rewarded.*

Scriptures: Matthew 10:42, 25:35-40; Mark 9:41, 12:41-44; I Corinthians 3:11-15.

Week 15
I KNOW HOW THEY BUCK NOW!

I thought my sides would split with laughter when the circuit riding preacher, to whom I was showing a house, started talking about the circuit for which he is responsible. He told me he had been preaching for eighteen years and added good-naturedly, "I've been riding them a long time now. I know how they buck!"

We all roared with laughter. His family, that was viewing the house with him, doubled over in hysterics with me.

Speaking from the other side of the pulpit, I can attest to the truth of his statement. We can sure buck!

How many preachers do you know that plan to quit every Monday? Many times, they hit the bottom, believing Sunday's message was the worst one they ever preached, and sure enough Brother So-and-So walked away mad as fire.

Reminds me of the story I heard about the man who didn't want to go to church on Sunday morning. As he argued with his wife about how he didn't like the people, couldn't stand the deacons, hated the youth pastor, she responded by saying, "But dear . . . you have to go. *You're* the preacher!"

Our former pastor in California retired after thirty-nine years of ministry in the same church! Believe me he had seen it all. Talk about bucking! No matter what he did, or how well he did it, there were those who would criticize. But he hung in there! He rode it out and the Lord blessed in mighty ways. Sometimes folks got mad and left in a huff . . . but he just kept on preaching.

Throughout the years, hundreds of young people sat under his faithful ministry. Under his guidance a bible school was started where young men and women trained for the work of the Lord. Today many of them are evangelists, pastors, missionaries, and church workers. What if he had given up on a bad Monday morning? It would have been easy to throw in the towel when people seemed determined to live in sin no matter how hard he preached, no matter how many hours he agonized in prayer, and no matter how fervently he pleaded with them to repent.

I remember many times how grieved he was over people who had begun the Christian race in earnest and then fell by the wayside. Oh, how his heart was broken, over and over with those who wanted to buck off all restraint and responsibility. Despite the disappointments he kept on, Sunday after Sunday, month after month, year after year.

Dear friend, if you're a pastor, youth worker, Sunday school teacher or missionary . . . DON'T QUIT! Ride it out! God sees your heart and knows it's broken over those who don't seem to want to take instruction. He has seen your tears over the backslidden in your charge. He knows your frustration, as those you teach seem to stay lukewarm, never seeming to give their all to the Lord.

Figure 23 – I Know How They Buck Now

As Charlie and I have ministered through the years, we have become very discouraged at times. We have been tempted to throw in the towel and quit reaching out to others. What's the use? Who really cares anyway? Why bother? Let's just care about *us*. Let the world go to Hell in a hand basket!

And then we would get a letter . . . a phone call . . . an e-mail; just a word of encouragement from the Lord to continue on . . . and so we would take a deep breath and press on.

To all our fellow laborers in the Gospel of Jesus Christ, just remember the results belong to the Lord. We need to be like the preacher friend I talked to so many years ago . . . determined to ride it out! We need to love people despite their faults and failures. After all, that's the way God loves us, even when we're bucking Him.

SCRIPTURES FOR MEDITATION
(Selah – think on these things)

MONDAY: *I will remember to find ways to encourage my pastor and his wife.*

Scriptures: Ecclesiastes 4:9-12; I Corinthians 9:7-14; 2 Corinthians 7:13; Hebrews 6:10.

TUESDAY: *I will remind myself that I am not alone and God has many servants who are faithful.*

Scriptures: Numbers 12:7; I Kings 19:4-18; Matthew 25:21; Romans 11:4; 2 Timothy 4:16-18.

WEDNESDAY: *I will live in such a way as to be an example and encouragement to others.*

Scriptures: Numbers 13:27-30; I Samuel 17: 32-37; Luke 10:29-37; Acts 4:13; I Timothy 4:12.

THURSDAY: *I will not be a quitter!*

Scriptures: Jeremiah 12:5; Luke 16:10; Galatians 5:7; Ephesians 6:10-13; Philippians 3:7-14.

FRIDAY: *I refuse to give in to discouragement because God has a plan for my life.*

Scriptures: I Samuel 2:8-9; 2 Kings 20:1-5; Psalm 42:1-8, 73:14-23; Jeremiah 1:17-19.

SATURDAY: *I will remember that eternal rewards outweigh any trials I may go through in this life.*

Scriptures: Genesis 5:21-24; 2 Kings 2:11; Matthew 17:1-5; Hebrews 11:32-40; Jude 1:14-15.

Figure 24 - Reaching Higher No Matter What!

Week 16
OLD AGE IS CURIOUS

One time, while on a flight to California, I watched an in-flight movie entitled, *The Curious Case of Benjamin Button*. The fantasy drama film was based on a short story written in 1921 by F. Scott Fitzgerald.

The movie begins at the end of World War I. A baby boy who has the appearance and physical maladies of an old man is born. The father, who is already distraught at the death of the baby's mother during childbirth, is horrified when he looks at the baby.

He grabs the bundled infant and dashes out of the house. As he runs through the streets of New Orleans it's obvious he's wondering what to do with the monster child. Finally, he deposits him on the doorstep of a nursing home.

A kind lady named Queenie who works in the home is unable to have children of her own; so, she takes the infant and raises him. The child, whom Queenie names Benjamin, grows up and becomes younger in strength and vitality while growing chronologically older. Needless to say, it's a curious take on growing older . . . or as in Benjamin Button's case, younger!

Hey! Have you ever known someone who was born old? I've known people like that. Not a Benjamin Button, but just old in their thinking. They're too old to learn a new skill, too old to go back to school, too old to go on an adventure. Instead, they feel like they've done their part in life, and they'll just let the younger ones do the job . . . or get the education . . . or go on that trip up Mt. Everest.

Recently I heard of a church where the old folks were letting the younger ones do the teaching, the nursery work and even helping with the cleaning of the church. "Oh, I've done my part. It's time for the younger ones to do that . . . haven't you heard? I've retired!"

This reminds me of two distinctly opposite characters in the Bible. The first is 80-year-old Barzillai. (lit. Son of Iron). King David asked Barzillai to come over to Jerusalem with him and live in his palace. The king assured him he would take care of him.

Not this old coot. He had a litany of excuses ranging from, I don't know how much longer I will live . . . I've lost my taster, can't hear well . . . I'll just go back home and look forward to being buried by mom and dad.

Well, have it your way Barzillai. Go back to what's comfortable and familiar. God forbid, don't consider any changes. You hate change. You would be better off sticking with the familiar, instead of the unknown, even if it's an invitation from the king (II Samuel 19:31-39).

Then there's Caleb (lit. bold). He's an 85-year old just itching for a very real adventure. Caleb is one of those men who never forgets anything; it's been over 40 years, but he hasn't forgotten a promise made to him by Moses.

Figure 25 – The Tucks as Mr. & Mrs. Noah

The leader of Israel told him he could have a particular mountain when they got to the Promised Land and he was ready to claim it . . . never mind that there were giants there. He was going to do a little kicking, but he was up to it. Get out of Caleb's way.

Caleb said, ". . . I am this day fourscore and five years old. As yet I am as strong this day as I was in the day that Moses sent me. Now therefore give me this mountain!" (Joshua 14:7-14)

My Charlie is a bit like old Caleb. At 84 he exercises regularly, keeps his mind sharp as a tack by reading his Bible and other reading materials and keeps active by going to church, attending the grandchildren's ball games and other activities and never fails to make the coffee for our morning wake up time! (HeBREWS!)

Well, it's curious for sure. One old person can be as set in their ways as an iron stake, never making a move. Others can be as bold as a lion and always heading upwards. I believe our attitude determines our altitude. What about you, friend. Are you stuck or moving up? I'm just curious.

SCRIPTURES FOR MEDITATION
(Selah – think on these things)

MONDAY: *I will not consider age a factor when serving or believing the Lord.*

Scriptures: Genesis 17:15-1, 21:1-7; Deuteronomy 33:24-25; Psalm 92:13-15; Ecclesiastes 12:1.

TUESDAY: *I will remember that God is more concerned with my heart than my outer looks.*

Scriptures: I Samuel 16:7; Proverbs 4:23, 31:29-31; Jeremiah 17:9-10; Matthew 12:34-35.

WEDNESDAY: *I will not make excuses for not doing what is right or for doing what is wrong.*

Scriptures: Genesis 1:6-13; Luke 14:16-24; Hebrews 4:12-13; James 4:17; Revelation 12:1-18.

THURSDAY: *I will not become lazy in my walk with the Lord.*

Scriptures: Psalm 1:1-2; Proverbs 6:6-11, 10:4-5; Matthew 13:24-25; Revelation 3:15-16.

FRIDAY: *I will remember that one person can make a difference.*

Scriptures: 2 Samuel 20:19-22; Esther 4:14; Ecclesiastes 9:13-15; Daniel 6:21-28; Acts 7:55-60.

SATURDAY: *I will keep a positive attitude today, knowing God is for me.*

Scriptures: Judges 6:12-14; I Samuel 24:15-20; Psalm 18:2, 118:17; Romans 8:33-39.

Week 17
GOING ONCE, GOING TWICE . . . SOLD!

I could hardly believe my eyes when I saw all the cars lined up on both sides of the highway and down an adjacent side street. What in the world? If there was a death in the family, the person sure did have a lot of friends and relatives. But, no . . . it was an auction. I can't remember seeing that many cars line a highway in Cochran since our house almost burned to the ground about 20 years ago.

Figure 26 - Going Once, Going Twice . . . SOLD!

According to one of my children, the auction was a huge success. It almost looked like a party was going on. For some an auction is more fun than a party. I'm sure the auctioneer was a happy camper when he counted up his profits at the end of the day.

Actually no one is really sure when auctions began. Earliest records indicate that they could go back as far as 500 B.C. At that time, women were auctioned to be wives. It was even considered illegal to allow a daughter to be "sold" outside the auction method.

Today, when you buy something at auction you're stuck with it, even if what you thought was valuable turns out to be junk. Back in the days when women were being sold, a buyer could get a return of money if he and his new spouse did not get along well; but unlike a horse, maidens could not be "tried" before auction.

Many years ago, we had a family reunion and for fun we took everyone to the Montrose auction. That was in the days before the auction house had fancy TV monitors to show off their goods and a central heating and cooling system to keep the buyers comfortable.

All of a sudden, I saw a painting I just had to have. A young maiden was sitting at a piano with her right hand raised in the air and her left hand on the keys. A look of rapture was on her sweet face. The bidding got higher and higher and finally it was mine!

When I saw it up close I was horrified. The painting was atrocious. I didn't realize her neckline was lower than proper and it was not an original. Everyone in our group laughed at my great purchase and someone dubbed her the "Pentecostal Hussy."

About three years later we had another family reunion and we had everyone put their name in a pot and we drew for a winner of a secret prize. You guessed it... my fantastic auction buy. Later one of my grandchildren, so disappointed that she wasn't the winner, came to me and said, "Grandma, how come all the names in the basket said Mary?"

Figure 27 - Going Once, Going Twice ... SOLD!

Well, Mary and her husband John hauled the Pentecostal Hussy off to California and ever since then, we have bounced the old painting back and forth from coast to coast. To tell the truth I'm not sure who has it right now, but you can be sure she will reappear at the next family reunion.

One of my favorite poems, written in 1921 by Myra Brooks Welch, is about an auction. It tells of an old battered and scarred violin. The auctioneer was having a terrible time getting someone to buy the ugly looking musical instrument. The final bid was a meager three dollars.

> "From the back of the room a gray-haired man came up and started playing the violin. When he finished, the auctioneer hit the gavel and began again... 'One thousand, one thousand, Do I hear two?' 'Two thousand; who makes it three?' 'Three thousand once, three thousand twice... going and gone,' said he."

"The audience cheered, But, some of them cried, 'We just don't understand.' What changed its worth?' Swift came the reply, 'The Touch of the Masters Hand.' And many a man with life out of tune, all battered with bourbon and gin, is auctioned cheap to a thoughtless crowd; much like that old violin. A mess of pottage, a glass of wine, a game and he travels on."

"He is going once, he is going twice, he is going and almost gone. But the Master comes, and the foolish crowd never can quite understand, the worth of a soul and the change that is wrought . . . by the Touch of the Master's Hand."

Those of us, who have been purchased by the blood of Christ, remember when we were on the auction block of sin. We were slaves to sin, but Jesus felt we were worth the price and so He bought us with His blood. By doing this He revealed how much He values us. Where are you today my friend . . . on the auction block of sin, or in the family of the Son of God?

SCRIPTURES FOR MEDITATION
(Selah – think on these things)

MONDAY: *I will not forget that I was once a slave to sin, but now I am free.*

Scriptures: Exodus 2:23-25, 14:21-31; John 8:31-36; Romans 6:20-23; Galatians 5:1.

TUESDAY: *I will be thankful that I have been redeemed by the blood of the Lamb.*

Scriptures: Exodus 12:12-14; Matthew 26:26-28; John 1:29; I Peter 1:18-19; Revelation 7:9-14.

WEDNESDAY: *I will be thankful that God considers me of great value, so much so, that He sent His Son to die for me.*

Scriptures: Isaiah 9:6-7, 53:3-10; Matthew 16:26; Luke 19:10; John 1:14-17; Galatians 4:3-7.

THURSDAY: *I will look at others through the eyes of God and realize every person has value.*

Scriptures: 2 Samuel 9:1-11; Ezekiel 16:4-9; Matthew 10:29-31, 18:1-6; Luke 17:12-19.

FRIDAY: *I will be a willing vessel to bless others, even when others have hurt me.*

Scriptures: Genesis 45:1-8; I Samuel 24:1-12; Matthew 6:7-15; Philemon 1:10-18; I Peter 3:8-11.

SATURDAY: *I will not allow my past to determine my future.*

Scriptures: Genesis 32:24-30; Zechariah 13:5-9; Acts 3:1-10; I Corinthians 6:11; 2 Corinthians 5:17.

Week 18
JOY IN THE JOURNEY

One of my favorite stories is about a precocious boy named Peter, who did not enjoy going to school, but instead loved to daydream his life away. One day an old woman appeared to him in the forest and offered him a golden ball, from which dangled a silver thread.

Peter discovered that by pulling on the thread he could make time pass by more quickly. What a delight to skip tests in school, zip through classes. Before he realized what was happening he had pulled so much of the magic thread that his mother was old and he was middle-aged!

The modern counterpart to The Magic Thread is a movie entitled Click. Actor Adam Sandler is given a universal remote and he finds that he can do the same thing Peter did. Before long he is an old man and has fast-forwarded his life away.

In both imagined instances, the key players wanted to rush past the unpleasant things in life and enjoy the fruits of their labors without expending any effort in the process. They were so busy looking for the destination they didn't enjoy the journey along the way.

I remember when our teenagers were growing up. They just couldn't wait until they were 15 so they could get their learner's permits. Then the magic age was 16 when they could get a driver's license. Soon a college degree was the goal, then marriage and now our oldest son is looking forward to retirement. How swiftly time goes by and if we're not careful we'll miss the enjoyment of the journey.

During my real estate career (1979-2007) I saw the span of mortgage interest rates fluctuate from 4.5 percent to 18.0 percent. I saw prices on land in our area jump from $1,000 an acre to $30,000 an acre. When I first started appraising property, the square foot price for a house was $20. Shortly before retiring it had jumped to $80+ a square foot!

Some interesting things happened while selling real estate. One time I was appalled to learn that a builder had used a 55-gallon drum for a septic tank. Another time a concerned buyer told me he had found a cemetery on his property. Gulp! Somehow that fact was overlooked both by an attorney and a surveyor during the closing process. Thankfully I was never sued or reprimanded by the Georgia Real Estate Commission during my real estate career. I give God the glory for this.

Figure 28 - Joy in the Journey

I also met people who have become lifelong friends. Some have found Jesus Christ as their personal Savior in my office. Some adopted Charlie and me and we've become surrogate parents and grandparents.

Being in real estate afforded me the opportunity to meet business and civic leaders and I learned firsthand what a great community we have here in Cochran. It's been ten years since I took a new turn in the journey called "life." Tuck Realty closed its doors for the final time and I entered the world of retirement.

I am determined to continue enjoying my journey through life. I am blessed with the best husband in the world and we are looking forward to more time than ever together.

Solomon gave some great advice in Ecclesiastes. "Go then, eat your bread in happiness . . . enjoy life with the woman whom you love all the days of our fleeting life . . . whatever your hand finds to do, verily, do it with all your might . . ." (Eccl. 9:7-10).

Chuck Swindoll put it succinctly in his book, *The Ragged Edge*: "If you are waiting to live it up when you're six feet under, pal, you're in for a major disappointment! The time to live is NOW. And the way to do it is to pull out all the stops and play full volume!"

I'm glad I've never had a golden ball with a magic thread or a universal remote to fast forward my life. Every day is an opportunity to live life to the fullest with Jesus. The joy in the journey comes when we put Jesus first, Others second and Yourself last. What a wonderful way to spell J.O.Y.

SCRIPTURES FOR MEDITATION

(Selah – think on these things)

MONDAY: *I will remember to have joy in my journey.*

Scriptures: I Kings 8:65-66; Nehemiah 8:10; Psalms 126:1-6; Proverbs 15:13-15, 17:22.

TUESDAY: *I will try to bring joy to others.*

Scriptures: Leviticus 25:35-36; Ruth 2:7-12; I Samuel 16:23; Isaiah 58:6-8; Luke 6:38; Acts 20:35.

WEDNESDAY: *I will do my best to make each day count for eternity.*

Scriptures: Psalm 23:6, 90:4-12, 118:24; Hebrews 12:1-3; I Peter 4:12-17.

THURSDAY: *I will remember that everything is subject to change but God.*

Scriptures: Psalm 102:25-27; Malachi 3:6; Matthew 24:25; Hebrews 13:8; 2 Peter 3:10.

FRIDAY: *I will encourage others in their journey through life.*

Scriptures: I Samuel 2:8-9; Job 22:23-29; Matthew 22:1-10; Acts 18:24-26.

SATURDAY: *I will remember that to put **J**esus first; **O**thers second and **Y**ourself last, spells **J.O.Y.**!*

Scriptures: I Chronicles 22:19; Psalms 16:8-9; Matthew 6:33; Mark 10:17-23; Romans 12:9-10.

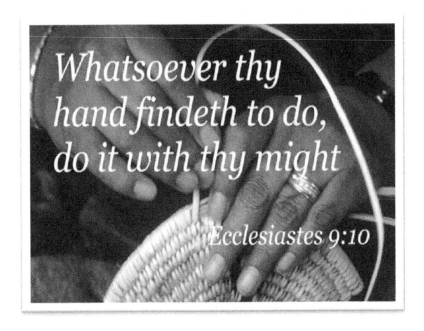

Figure 29 - Ecclesiastes 9:10

Week 19
LOVE LETTERS

Shortly after Charlie and I were engaged I went on a mission trip to Mexico. During that time, we wrote to one another and those letters from Charlie are still so special to me. I usually untie the now faded ribbon and reread them on our anniversary. Since we've been married, we've been able to share our feelings of love personally or by cell phone when apart.

Imagine my surprise when I went to a ladies' retreat and one of the coordinators, standing before us with a batch of odd-shaped envelopes, said she had a surprise for all of us.

As she began to pass them out I realized they were letters from the husbands. Tears began to flow, as women opened and read the special words of love from their honeys.

I watched and waited. Where was my letter? Didn't Charlie write to me? I began to get a little panicky, but decided I would be blasé if he didn't send one and just rejoice for the others who were reading theirs.

Finally, Kellie handed me a letter, apologizing that she didn't know who it belonged to because it began with the words, "My Darling . . ." and then it ended with: "All my love, C." Charlie had not placed it in an envelope. When she realized I was the only one without a letter she figured it out.

I know you're wondering what he said. Sorry. It was for my eyes only! I can say that I sure wasn't disappointed with the contents and now I have another letter to add to the pile that is nearly 45 years old!

After reading my letter I wondered what the single ladies had received. It wasn't long before one of my friends shared her letter with me and I've asked her if I could pass it on.

"Dearest JoAnn, It was very early this morning, 6:37 a.m. to be exact, that I was admiring the sun as it slowly began to break through the clouds. It was truly majestic. In a small way the daybreak reminded me of you. (I say in a small way because the beauty of the daybreak pales in the light of you.)

"I'm sure you're wondering about my identity . . . is this some freaky secret admirer? No, not at all, I mean, I'm not freaky, but I am an admirer. I've actually admired you for, well, a long time. I just wanted you to know that I think about you all the time; and I do mean all the time. There is, in fact, not a moment that you are not flittering across my mind.

"Let me just go ahead and give you the essence of my feelings toward you . . . I love you immensely! My love for you transcends any form of measurement on earth. I can't help myself. Whoops, there goes my identity right, but that's ok. I never said that I was a 'secret' admirer.

"I am the one who gave you the breath of life, formed you in your mother's womb and I even named you. (You will love your new name . . . I promise). I have such awesome plans for you. I want you to have a great time at this retreat and know for sure that you will leave with

Figure 30 - Love Letters

not only what you came for . . . but more. Remember, I love you sooooo much!

"P.S. After this is over I would really like to spend some 'One on one' quality time with you. I have some specific plans and expectations that I am anxious to share with you. With All My Love . . . GOD!"

I didn't read anyone else's letter, but if they were anything like mine and JoAnn's they were awesome.

All of us are in possession of God's special love letters. The Bible contains such words of encouragement, comfort, and affirmation. We are so special to the Lord. Every day He thinks of us. He tells us that His thoughts toward us are more than can be numbered (Psalm 139). You might say He's wild about us!

He tells us we're his betrothed, His bride-to-be. He's preparing the wedding suite right now and when the time is right we will see Him face to face. Are you in love with Him? Are you reading His love letters to you?

SCRIPTURES FOR MEDITATION
(Selah – think on these things)

MONDAY: *I will always keep Jesus as my "first love."*

Scriptures: Genesis 24:64-67; Song of Solomon 1:1-4; Jeremiah 31:3; John 15:9-14; Revelation 2:4-5.

TUESDAY: *I will never doubt God's enduring love for me.*

Scriptures: Song of Solomon 8:6-7; Hosea 14:1-4; Romans 5:8, 8:35-39; I John 4:7-10.

WEDNESDAY: *I will remember that true love requires sacrifice.*

Scriptures: Genesis 22:1-14; Deuteronomy 10:12; 2 Samuel 24:21-25; John 15:9-13; I Thessalonians 1:1-4.

THURSDAY: *I will remember that God's love far surpasses man's love.*

Scriptures: Deuteronomy 7:6-18; Isaiah 49: 14-16; Jonah 4:1-11; Luke 23:32-46; Romans 5:1-8.

FRIDAY: *I will let God love others through me.*

Scriptures: 2 Kings 4:8-17; Luke 10: 29-37; Acts 16:26-34; 2 Timothy 1:16-18; Hebrews 6:10.

SATURDAY: *I will remember that charity (God's love) endures forever.*

Scriptures: Proverbs 8:17; John 3:16; Romans 8:37-39; I Corinthians 13:1-13; Revelation 1:4-5.

Week 20

THE WORLD IS A DANGEROUS PLACE

Aside from the obvious events chronicled daily by the various news media, the world around the Tuck place has also been known to be dangerous.

It wasn't long after Alan (our surrogate son) and his friend Brandon, cut down umpteen trees by mistake, that Alan tried to redeem himself by saving one of the trees that had been overtaken by a wild scuppernong vine.

When I arrived home late that afternoon he was on top of a tall ladder with bow saw in hand. I yelled, "Alan, what in the world are you doing up there?" He replied that he was going to save this particular tree from destruction.

I commented that his method of conservation looked pretty dangerous as he lifted up his tee shirt to proudly display his scraped chest and pointed out his skinned-up arms. Undaunted by these minor injuries he was determined to climb up the tree again and cut off the choking vines.

I just shook my head and went into the house. I couldn't watch so I tried the old method of "out of sight-out of mind." Hours later he came into the house, changed clothes, and headed to the local supermarket, where his REAL JOB was located. I, along with Charlie, planned to go to bed early that night since Charlie was scheduled for a stress test in Macon the following morning.

The stress test turned out to be the precursor for a quick wheelchair ride from the doctor's office to the Macon Medical Center where a stent was installed in one of Charlie's arteries that was 90 percent blocked.

As we sat in Charlie's hospital room, waiting for the results of the stent installation, we got a call from Alan, telling me he had a really bad day. What now?

It seems those vines were determined to get the best of Alan and all the cutting in the world wouldn't get them to release their grip. That's when he decided to put a rope around the vines and pull them down. As he was pulling, he kept hearing a strange noise. In his words, it sounded as if the tree was falling, like it had been cut.

However, the noise turned out to be the rattling sound of a four-foot long rattlesnake, instead of a tree falling. Alan said he froze for a minute and so did the snake. When the snake stopped rattling; Alan tore out of the field like a ruptured duck.

Figure 31 - The World is a Dangerous Place

Oh, but that wasn't the end of Paul Bunyan's story. He climbed into Babe (our old blue Nissan truck) and headed for the dump with a load of brush and vines. That's where Babe died.

After many attempts to push the truck off and get it started, Alan looked under the hood and somehow managed to get shocked so bad that he thought he had been electrocuted! (He was a bit gun-shy of electricity since he was seriously shocked a few years prior.)

Picking himself up off the ground he slammed down the hood, gave the truck another push, and he flew out of the dump, went into the house, and gave up yard work for the day.

I'm glad to report that he survived his whole ordeal, as did Charlie with his stent installation. Life was back to normal again and I was reminded again of the goodness of God.

I'm so glad Alan wasn't bitten by that snake and that Charlie made it in time to the hospital before a heart attack got him. Because of all the blessings we enjoyed that particular week I certainly gave the Lord praise for His loving care of the Tuck family. Giving God praise is something we do every single day!

When we hear of terrorist bombings, kids getting beaten in school buses by bullies, and murders taking place in upscale neighborhoods, we need to realize that a dangerous place could be right in our own backyards. In times like these it's good to know that the Lord is our only insurance against the plans that Satan has to destroy us.

One of the verses in the Bible that has been especially dear to us through the years is found in Isaiah 54:17 which states, "No weapon formed against you shall prosper." And of course, you realize that I don't own that verse. Those words of encouragement are for ALL of us.

SCRIPTURES FOR MEDITATION
(Selah – think on these things)

MONDAY: *I will not fear, for the Lord is with me.*

Scriptures: Exodus 14:13-14; Deuteronomy 20:1-4; 2 Kings 6:15-17; Isaiah 41:10; Luke 12:4-7.

TUESDAY: *I will remember that in the middle of any danger the Lord is with me.*

Scriptures: I Samuel 17:32-37, 47-51; Isaiah 43:1-2; Daniel 3:23-27, 6:16-22; Acts 27:22-25.

WEDNESDAY: *I will use wisdom in all matters.*

Scriptures: Psalm 90:12; Proverbs 1:1-7, 4:4-7, 16:16, 29:15; James 1:5.

THURSDAY: *I will extend grace to others realizing I am not perfect.*

Scriptures: 2 Samuel 9:1-9; Ecclesiastes 7:20; Luke 6:30-38, 15:11-24; John 8:3-11; Romans 3:23.

FRIDAY: *I will praise the Lord in the good times and in the bad times.*

Scriptures: Job 1:20-22; Psalm 34:1, 113:1-3; Acts 16:23-26; 2 Corinthians 11: 22-31.

SATURDAY: *I will pray for my family's protection and take comfort that they are in God's hand.*

Scriptures: Genesis 18:17-19; Joshua 14:9-13; I Samuel 1:19-28; Psalms 128:1-6; Proverbs 31:21.

Week 21

AN APPOINTMENT WITH DEATH

The other day as I was driving home on the Interstate, I moved into the left lane to keep from going into downtown Macon. Passing me in the right lane was a motorcycle rider. I got a real shock when I glanced at him. He was wearing a mask, but it wasn't a typical motorcycle mask . . . it was a mask that looked like the death angel!

He turned to look in my direction as he exited the interstate to Macon. The mask, which looked like a smiling skull, was no doubt put on to do exactly what it did, bring shock value!

As I continued toward home, I couldn't help but think about a story told in the Arabian Nights about Death's visit to a bazaar.

At the bazaar was a man shopping for the latest bargain. He looked up from a table of goods and saw death; he was robed in black and had a scythe in his hand. (No doubt his face looked like the mask of the bike rider I had seen on the Interstate.)

Terrified, the man mounted his horse and traveled as fast as he could to the next village. Relieved that he was in another and supposedly safe location; he went to the local bazaar and continued his shopping.

Who should confront him once again, Death! Shaking from head to toe, the man stood there in abject terror. Death looked at him somberly and said, "We have an appointment today in this village and when I saw you at the other village I wondered if you would make it in time."

Life and death are not in our hands, but in the hands of our Creator. Each week Charlie and I read the obituaries in our local paper and jokingly say, "Nope. Not our turn this week."

Man strives to hold onto life, but the statistics have always shown that 100 out of 100 die. No matter what you do, no matter how much you have, and no matter who you know, you're not getting out of this life alive.

For the last several days I've been noticing a little spider making his home on one of our outside lights. I keep thinking that I need to wipe the web down and get rid of that little pest, but instead I've just kept watching the web grow . . . and watching the spider work.

Yesterday I was reading a verse in Proverbs that says, "The spider skillfully grasps with its hands and is in kings' palaces" (Prov. 30:28).

Figure 32 – An Appointment with Death

Have you noticed how a spider is comfortable just about any place? Whether in the Tuck house or in a king's palace, a spider gets along just fine. That is, until someone takes a broom or a rag and wipes out its little home.

It's amazing how the little spider thinks that all is well in the web of his making. Surrounded by amazing wealth and beauty . . . all is well with the spider in the king's palace . . . but in a moment of time, he is gone and so is his house.

Sometimes we're like the spider, spinning our webs, not thinking that in a moment everything could come crashing down around us and we could be in eternity.

Recently a friend was taken to the hospital. The diagnosis was a stroke. He felt the web of his secure little world crashing down on him. For years he had held everyone at arm's length. No prayer for him. He didn't need anyone other than himself . . . that is, until he faced his own mortality . . . until he was staring The Grim Reaper in the face.

I'm happy to report that my friend is doing well physically and spiritually. He met the giver of spiritual life in the emergency room that day. Instead of turning Jesus away, as he had so many times before, he invited him into his heart and life.

Friend, our world is like a spider's web. On the world scene, we see nations in turmoil; on the financial scene we see nothing ahead but a bankrupt economy. Morally, our country is in free fall with basic standards of conduct out the window and a philosophy of "anything goes" permeating our educational institutions.

Your web may be in a king's palace or in a small three-bedroom home in the suburbs, but one day your appointment will come . . . and then what? "It's appointed unto men once to die and after this the judgment" (Hebrews 9:27).

SCRIPTURES FOR MEDITATION
(Selah – think on these things)

MONDAY: *I will remember that 'life is short – death is sure – sin the cause – Christ the cure'!*

Scriptures: Genesis 3:1-4; Psalm 34:4-5; Isaiah 57:1; Romans 5:12; I Peter 1:24-25; I John 1:7-10.

TUESDAY: *I will stay on the right path, for it leads to everlasting life.*

Scripture: Deuteronomy 30:19-20; I Kings 18:21; Proverbs 4:18; Isaiah 26:7, 35:8-10; John 14:1-6.

WEDNESDAY: *Regardless of what the world situation may be, I am trusting my God and He will not fail.*

Scriptures: Psalm 46:1-3, 56:3-11, 139:1-12; John 10:27-29, 16:33; Hebrews 13:5-8; Revelation 3:10-11.

THURSDAY: *I will not become self-confident or compromising in this world, realizing that death or the return of the Lord can happen at any moment.*

Scriptures: Matthew 24:44-51, 25:1-13; Mark 8:34-38; Acts 5:27-29; I Corinthians 1:1-58; James 4:4.

FRIDAY: *I will remember that death or life is in the Lord's hands, not mine!*

Scriptures: Ecclesiastes 3:1-3; Daniel 5:24-31; Amos 5:14-19; John 19:7-11; Hebrews 9:27.

SATURDAY: *I am determined to live my life in such a way that I will bring honor to my God.*

Scriptures: Exodus 32:26; Proverbs 10:7, 11:10; Luke 9:57-62; Acts 7:55-60; 2 Timothy 4:6-8.

Week 22

BINGO!

In case you don't know about the Goodwill Industries store in Macon, you're missing a great used bookstore. Every now and then, when Charlie and I are in that neck of the woods, we check out the latest deals!

The other day I found a book by author Richard Booker, entitled *The Miracle of the Scarlet Thread*. Since I had been doing research on this particular subject for an upcoming bible study, I was thrilled to add another commentary to our library.

I was intrigued by the personal note written on the backside of the front cover, which read in part, "Mitchell . . . this is one of the finest books I have found on the subject, 'covenant.' It is one of my top ten or so Christian books. I hope it will be a blessing and welcome addition to your library also."

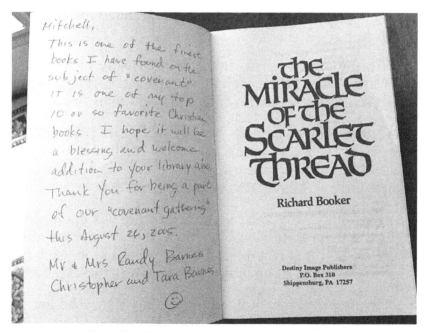

Figure 33 - The Miracle of the Scarlet Thread - Bingo!

The donor signed his name, but that was all. I read it to Charlie and commented, "I wish I knew who this person is and where he's from. What a nice gift to give someone." Those of us who are book lovers just naturally think; a good book is the best gift in the world.

The book still had that new feel to it and I was glad it wasn't all marked up like some used books are. (I'm notorious for marking in books; but I don't like it when I see other people's markings – go figure!)

As I continued reading through the book night after night, I had to agree with the donor. The book does an outstanding job in tying together the loose ends of the blood covenant as set forth in the Bible.

One evening I turned a page and BINGO! There, hidden between pages 70 and 71, was a personal check for $40. Obviously, Mitchell never read the book because the check written in 2005 had not been cashed.

Sorry Mitchell. You not only missed the blessings contained in the explanations and teachings of Richard Booker, but you also missed the monetary blessing intended for you by the donor.

To me the book was not only a treasure of words, but when I found that little check I was once again reminded that blessings come to those who diligently seek them.

How many of us miss the blessings that God Almighty has for us in His Holy Word? Instead of reading it, we leave it on the coffee table or night stand to gather dust. How many treasures have we missed this week, last month or even all year?

Hopefully we haven't gone as far as to box up our bibles and donate them to the local Goodwill Industries. I'm always amazed at how many bibles line the shelves of used book stores. Who owned these bibles and why were they discarded?

While in Warner Robins last week we stopped and visited another favorite used book store, Gottwalls. They have a fantastic selection including, among other subjects, Christian titles, the classics, and everything you might want to read about the Civil War (one of Charlie's favorites). Again, there was shelf after shelf of new and old Bibles.

Some say they don't understand the Bible and think reading it is a waste of time and effort. Oh, but if they only knew the author personally, it would be a different story.

Others complain that the Bible is a boring book and having read it once, think that's quite enough. However, I contend there are treasures (better than a $40 check) tucked away on the pages of Holy Writ. There's one slight catch. The treasures are reserved for those who are seeking them.

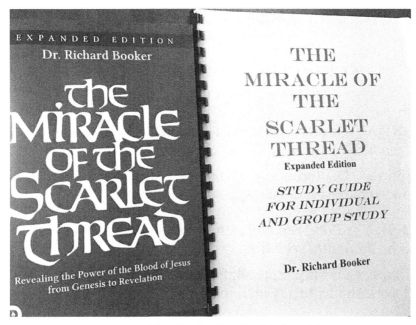

Figure 34 - The Miracle of the Scarlet Thread #2

Jesus put it this way: "Every scribe who has been trained for the kingdom of heaven is like the master of a house, who brings out of his treasure what is new and what is old" (Matthew 13:52). The truths we find may be old or new to us, but amazingly we can never plumb the depths of the treasures contained in God's Word.

By the way, it took a little detective work, but I finally found the donors of the little book. Their phone number had been changed in the last seven years, but they still lived at the same address.

When Mrs. Donor discovered that her husband had written the check, she was not one bit surprised. "My husband is such a giver," she declared. "He's always giving away money!"

I answered, "That's great. He's just like God . . . a giver." "On the other hand," I thought, "Mitchell was the loser." How about us? Are we losing out today because we're not searching?

"It is the glory of God to conceal a thing: but the honor of kings is to search out a matter" (Proverbs 25:2).

SCRIPTURES FOR MEDITATION
(Selah – think on these things)

MONDAY: *I will be diligent to search the Scriptures for the treasures contained therein.*

Scriptures: Deuteronomy 17:14-20; 2 Kings 22:8-13; Psalm 19:7-11; Matthew 13:45-52.

TUESDAY: *I will remember that blessings will come to those who diligently seek God.*

Scripture: Genesis 32:24-28; Psalm 63:1; Isaiah 26:8-9, 55:1-7; I Corinthians 14:1; Galatians 6:7-9.

WEDNESDAY: *I will not miss out on hearing these words: "Well done, good and faithful servant."*

Scriptures: Matthew 10:42, 25:14-23; Mark 9:41; 2 Timothy 4:8; Revelation 2:7, 17, 26-27; 3:5, 12, 21.

THURSDAY: *I will remember that reading the Bible is never a waste of time.*

Scriptures: Job 23:12; Psalm 90:12, 119:9-11, 105; Jeremiah 23:29; John 17:17; 2 Timothy 3:14-17.

FRIDAY: *I will give to others as giving to the Lord.*

Scriptures: 2 Chronicles 15:7; Mark 12:29-31, 14:2-9; Luke 6:27-38; 2 Corinthians 9:7; Hebrews 6:10.

SATURDAY: *I will be aware that some of the biggest blessings may come in unexpected ways.*

Scriptures: Genesis 41:14-43, 45:7-8; Ruth 2:10-12; 1 Samuel 25:32-42; Luke 23:32-43; Acts 9:1-18.

Figure 35 - The Honor of Kings to Search out a Matter

Week 23

CAST YOUR BREAD UPON THE WATERS

Back in the '70s I used to pick up hitchhikers. Times were different then. There wasn't as much meanness going on. My motive was not only to be helpful, but also to tell them about Jesus. Sometimes I would bring them home and feed them a good home cooked meal before taking them back to the road, or perhaps to their destination.

The last person I brought home was a young man, who turned out to be A.W.O.L. That did it! Charlie said, "No more hitchhikers, honey. I know you mean well, but someone could hurt you or, as in this case, you could even go to jail for aiding and abetting a fleeing soldier."

I was sad about this turn of events, but in my heart, I knew Charlie was right. I knew I could lift up a prayer for hitchhikers when I saw them. God would find a way to reach them with His love, even if I couldn't.

One evening I was driving home when I saw two young men near a little convenience store. You guessed it. They were hitchhiking.

I stopped to ask where they were going and when they told me Savannah I exclaimed: "You'll never make it to Savannah from Cochran at this time of the night!"

I made a quick telephone call from a phone booth. Charlie was emphatic. "No! You can't bring them home!" Shucks!

"Guys, my husband thinks you're going to do something bad to me so I can't take you home, but I'll be right back."

I went straight to my friend Eleanor Mathews' house and told her my dilemma. She was kind enough to give me some money to finance a night at a local motel for the men. (This was back in the day when we were so poor we couldn't "pay attention.")

Figure 36 - Cast Your Bread Upon the Waters

Instructing them where to spend the night I gave them the money and also my Bible. Since I didn't have any tracts or other literature to give them I suggested they read everything I had underlined. Assuring me they would send it back, they were on their way. I sent up a silent prayer that God would reveal Himself to them.

Three weeks later Charlie asked, "Honey, where is your Scofield Bible?" "Uh, remember those two hitchhikers?" Needless to say, he was a bit upset with me.

Well, we weathered that situation with some smiles, hugs and with Charlie shaking his head in disbelief at me. I knew he was thinking, "What am I going to do with her?"

About a year later I was praying for a need that required ten dollars. Back then we prayed in every dime and each time God answered our prayers; faith just kept growing.

I went to the mailbox that morning and was surprised to find a package. When I opened it I was amazed to find my old Scofield Bible, a thank you note and TEN DOLLARS.

Don't you know I just hated to say, "I told you so?"

Fast forward to 2017 and I'm here to tell you that the same God Who blessed us with $10 back in the '70s, is the same God Who is blessing and providing for us today!

Recently I received a telephone call from a lady, whom I barely knew. "Mrs. Tuck," she began, "I just sold some property and I want to sow into your prison ministry."

To say I was excited was beyond an understatement, especially when she told me she was going to give me $1,000. I knew exactly what I was going to do with that money. We had already taught two Hebrew classes at our local detention center and now I would have the money to teach another one! (Materials are not cheap these days!)

I told her to make the check out to our church so she could receive an income tax deduction for her gift. The next day I went by to pick it up and a fellow worker of hers said she was at lunch, but that she had left a card for me.

I didn't want anyone to think I would mess with this dear woman's offering, so I didn't open the envelope. As it turned out, it was my husband's turn that evening to help the treasurer count the church offering. What a surprise I got when he told me the lady gave "over and above," and her offering for the prison ministry was a whopping $1,500!

Through these many years we have seen the Lord provide over and over again, for our needs, and ministries and sometimes even our wants. He is a God Who owns the cattle on a thousand hills.

I like to put it this way: Tithers are "Survivors," but those who give over and above are *"Thrivers."*

"Cast your bread upon the waters, for you will find it after many days" (Ecclesiastes 11:1).

SCRIPTURES FOR MEDITATION
(Selah – think on these things)

MONDAY: *I'll do what I can to help others in need.*

Scriptures: Genesis 24:10-20; I Kings 17:8-16; Proverbs 19:17, 31:10-20; Acts 9:36-42.

TUESDAY: *I will do my best to remember that my husband is the head of our house and honor him.*

Scripture: Ecclesiastes 4:9-12; Song of Solomon 8:4-7; Amos 3:3; Ephesians 5:21-24; I Peter 3:1-6.

WEDNESDAY: *I will lean on God's wisdom when I am dealing with the lost, knowing they are capable of incredible evil.*

Scriptures: 2 Chronicles 1:7-12; Matthew 10:16; Romans 1:26-32; I Corinthians 1:30-31; I John 4:1-6.

THURSDAY: *I will put God first in my giving, remembering the tithe belongs to the Lord.*

Scriptures: Genesis 14:18-20, 28:10-22; Deuteronomy 14:22-28; Malachi 3:8-11; Hebrews 7:1-10.

FRIDAY: *I am confident in God's promises to supply all my needs.*

Scriptures: I Kings 17:1-16; Matthew 6:25-34, 14:15-21; Ephesians 3:20; Philippians 4:11-19.

SATURDAY: *I will remember that the best treasures are those which are laid up in Heaven.*

Scriptures: Matthew 6:19-21; I Corinthians 3:11-15; Hebrews 11:24-26; I John 2:15-17; Revelation 21:1-7.

Just Jerri

Week 24
ARE YOU FOR REAL?

I just love living in a small town. Sometimes my husband is reluctant to see me go into the store for just one or two items because it might be an hour before I make it back home. The primary reason for my delay is because of all the visiting I have to do with folks at the meat counter, the canned goods aisle and at the bakery/deli.

One time I was approached by a stranger who inquired, "Are you the reality lady?"

Chuckling a little I responded by saying, "Yes, and I'm the realty lady too." The man was inquiring about a house I had for sale. He had recognized me from an advertisement for real estate in our local newspaper. After we talked about real estate for a few minutes (maybe more like 15 minutes) we went our separate ways, but I began to ponder his "reality" mis-speak.

Webster defines reality as "the quality or state of being real." Today, there are many plastic people that we meet every day. On the outside everything appears to be fine, but on the inside, they are full of multiple emotions ranging from anger to disappointment.

The youth in our church did a skit one time portraying plastic people. The skit brought home the truth of the words in a Christian song, a portion of which goes like this: "Fairy tales and dreams, I want to know reality. Keep my heart from blindness, so I can clearly see, I want to know reality."

Figure 37 - Are You for Real?

Young people today are not the only ones looking for the real thing. I rub shoulders everyday with people looking for answers and not just empty platitudes. The young single mother who is struggling to hold things together with a "barely-making it-income" needs help. We can sing, "It Is Well with My Soul," but is our neighbor struggling to pay a utility bill? Is our Christianity real?

Can we be real enough to say we're hurting? On a recent Sunday morning, a friend was leaving church and she looked a bit downcast. When I asked her if everything was okay, her eyes filled with tears. Everything was NOT okay and she was real enough to admit she needed prayer for a need in her family.

Later that evening a small group of us gathered to pray with this family about the problem. By Saturday of the following week they experienced an incredible answer to our prayers. Their prodigal had come home.

Had my friend put on a plastic smile we would not have been able to bear the burden with her. It's okay to say we're hurting. It's okay to say we're sick. It's okay to admit we're having problems with temptation. If we can't be real with our Christian family, then how are we ever going to experience the victory that comes when we pray for one another?

In his book, *What's So Amazing About Grace?* author Philip Yancey writes, "I realize that imperfection is the prerequisite for grace. Light only gets in through the cracks."

Many years ago (more than I care to remember), I was so discouraged and defeated about a situation. As I left church that morning my pastor shook my hand and said, "Is everything okay?" I just smiled a plastic smile, but at the same time I muttered, "No, everything is terrible."

The following morning, he was at my door. His encouragement and confidence in me caused me to make the right choice in a difficult decision I was facing.

Being real is not always easy. Sometimes we have to admit we've made mistakes; that we've taken wrong turns, that we haven't always taken the high road and lived as God wanted; but being real is vital to our growth as Christians.

When we're real we can receive forgiveness because we can face our sins. When we're real we can learn where we can improve. We can quit hiding behind the façade of plastic smiles and let people know we need help.

Hey, are you the reality lady . . . the reality man?

"This poor man cried and the LORD heard him and saved him out of all his troubles" (Psalms 34:6).

SCRIPTURES FOR MEDITATION

(Selah – think on these things)

MONDAY: *I refuse to be a hypocrite.*

Scriptures: Job 8:10-14, 27:8-10; Proverbs 11:9; Isaiah 33:13-17; Matthew 6:1-6; Luke 13:13-17.

TUESDAY: *I will take care to guard my heart so my words will glorify God.*

Scripture: Proverbs 4:20-23, 15:28; Matthew 12:34-37, 15:7-11; Luke 6:43-45; 2 Timothy 2:22.

WEDNESDAY: *I will be sensitive to the Holy Spirit's leading, knowing that many hide their hurts, afraid of rejection by others.*

Scriptures: Psalm 30:11-12, 42:5-11, 43:1-5; Isaiah 58:10-12, 61:1-3; Matthew 23:37; Ephesians 4:32.

THURSDAY: *I will try to live as an example of Christ before others.*

Scriptures: 2 Corinthians 5:17-21; Colossians 1:27-29; I Timothy 4:12; 2 Timothy 3:10-15; Jude 1:20-25.

FRIDAY: *I will remember there is power in praying with other believers.*

Scriptures: Deuteronomy 32:30; Daniel 2:13-18, 27-28; Matthew 18:19-20; Acts 12:5-12.

SATURDAY: *I will remember that God is not looking for perfection, but for progress.*

Scriptures: Ecclesiastes 7:20; Isaiah 6:1-8, 64:6; Jeremiah 17:9-10; Luke 18:9-14; I John 1:9.

Week 25
DO YOU HAVE A BEEPER?

I am so thankful for a car that regularly beeps me. A few years ago, I picked up my sweet young friend, Jasmin Allen to take her and my granddaughter to the movies. Just as I was heading up the street to my granddaughter's house my ten-mile gas warning beeper went off. Oops! I immediately changed directions and headed for the nearest gas station.

When we arrived at the theater to see the movie (*CARS*), I started to get out of my car and my ignition beeper went off. I almost left my keys in the vehicle. I laughingly told Jasmin and Mallory that the last half of the 20th Century has been, and no doubt the entire 21st Century, will be filled with beeps!

If we leave our refrigerator door open more than three minutes we get beeped. My dishwasher tells me when the dishes are done by beeping me. My stove beeps me, as does my answering machine and my clothes dryer. Everywhere I turn I'm getting beeped.

Now, Charlie doesn't hear all these beeps like I do. Working around aircraft engines and then as a gyro mechanic for years, caused him to suffer significant hearing loss. Sometimes I think he has selective hearing. My hearing, on the other hand, is so sharp that one night as I was lying in bed, I kept hearing a beep outside.

The sound was driving me nuts; so, I threw on my bathrobe, turned on the porch light and headed out the front door. Finally, I found the source of the beeping. A smoke alarm that I had put in our garage because the batteries were dead, was begging for a refill. Beep! Beep!

I'm sure if you let your mind wander for a minute you'll be able to think of many other sources of beeps that are in your life.

The Holy Spirit in the life of a Christian beeps us often. Sometimes we listen and sometimes we choose to ignore his gentle beep. Actually, my car had beeped me at the 50-mile danger zone, and then again at the 25-mile danger zone. I chose to ignore the first two warnings and almost ran out of gas.

Elijah, the great prophet of the Old Testament, learned firsthand about the beep of God. The Bible says the old prophet was all alone in a cave having a real pity party because of life's troubles. Suddenly a violent wind came up, then an earthquake, and then a fire. God didn't speak through any of these events, but instead came to Elijah in a still, small voice.

People have asked me the question, "How do you hear from God? How do you know when He is speaking to you?"

I think the key to hearing the spiritual beeps as alerts, is spending a lot of time reading His Word, the Bible. We get to know Him personally when we spend time in His Word. Jesus and the Word are one and the same.

Figure 38 – WARNING: Low Fuel!

"In the beginning was the Word, and the Word was with God, and the Word was God. The same was in the beginning with God. And the Word was made flesh and dwelt among us and we beheld His glory, the glory as of the only begotten of the Father, full of grace and truth" (John 1:1-2, 14).

Jesus IS the Word. As we read the Bible, we get to know Him and what His will is regarding life and death. We see His will regarding human suffering. We see His compassion toward the unlovely. We know how He feels about sin and righteousness.

When we hear His still, small voice talking to us we just KNOW it is Him because we have been spending time with Him. He said, "My sheep hear My voice, and I know them, and they follow Me" (John 10:27).

We need to be consciously wearing a beeper in our hearts every minute of the day. Don't wait until you run out of gas and are stalled somewhere out in the country with no help in sight. Listen to the warning beep!

SCRIPTURES FOR MEDITATION
(Selah – think on these things)

MONDAY: *I will remember the Lord is still speaking to men today, even as He did in days of old.*

Scriptures: Numbers 23:9; Joshua 24:24; I Samuel 3:1-10, 15:22; I Kings 19:11-12; Isaiah 30:15, 21.

TUESDAY: *I am grateful that God speaks to me every day.*

Scripture: 2 Samuel 22:7-14; Psalm 141:1-2; Jeremiah 20:9; John 16:12-14; Hebrews 1:1-2.

WEDNESDAY: *I am glad my Savior goes with me through every trial I may encounter.*

Scriptures: Numbers 20:16; Deuteronomy 31:6-8; 2Chronicles 14:10-12; Psalm 23:1-6, 34:15-20; Isaiah 43:2.

THURSDAY: *I am so thankful the Lord has made plain the path of righteousness.*

Scriptures: I Samuel 12:23-24; Psalm 119:105; Proverbs 2:3-9, 4:18; Isaiah 26:3-8, 30:21; Mark 1:17-18.

FRIDAY: *I refuse self-pity, for I know God is for me!*

Scriptures: Exodus 14:10-14; Psalm 124:1-8; Acts 20:22-24; Romans 8:28-31; Hebrews 13:5-6.

SATURDAY: *I will remember that the Holy Spirit is my helper and my teacher.*

Scriptures: Matthew 3:11; John 14:16-18, 26; Acts 1:1-8, 2:1-4; Romans 8:26-27; Jude 1:20-21.

Week 26
THE FUTURE LOOKS GOOD

Years ago I was intrigued when a real estate client told me that he and a group of his buddies met together every other Sunday to play marbles at the Hillside Family Campground right here in Cochran! Marbles? Wow! I thought the game of marbles was a thing of the past. How wrong I was. In searching the Internet, I discovered that marble playing, once relegated to little kids on dusty playgrounds, is big stuff nowadays.

Figure 39 – Grit Newsboy

The first National Marbles Tournament was held in 1922 and in June of 2017 the participants actually played 1,200 games over a four-day period. National honors, college scholarships, and numerous other prizes and awards were earned.

The American Marble Tournament (formerly Mountaineer Marble Tournament) was organized in 1990. Players, mostly from Charlie's home state of West Virginia, were the initial participants.

In recent years the tournament has grown to include participants from 19 different countries. The group that meets in Cochran is called the Grit Marble Club. Chuck Walker, one of the members, said they named it after the old-time country newspaper, "Grit."

Some folks in Cochran will remember the days when Jazzbo's Country Store was an icon in our little town. Back in the '70s we purchased our weekly Grit newspaper there. My, wasn't life uncomplicated back then?

I think the members of the Grit Marble Club, along with Charlie and I, long for those simple days when we didn't have to worry about terrorists blowing up buildings and having to warn our children about child molesters and kidnappers. I remember when our children would play in the woods behind our house for hours and I never gave their safety a second thought. It's just the way life was back then.

As for the old Grit newspaper, it is currently being published in a different format, but still with the simple, rural lifestyle in mind. When the first headline for Grit was set in 1882, it's doubtful anyone envisioned the publication continuing into the 21st century.

Dietrick Lamade was a 23-year-old assistant press foreman for the Williamsport, Pennsylvania, newspaper, The Daily Sun and Banner. In December 1882, the newspaper began a Saturday edition titled Grit, which included local news items, editorials and humorous tidbits. Lamade set the first headline for the new edition.

In 1885 Lamade bought the paper and in 1891 hit upon an idea of having newsboys sell Grit directly to the public. The newspaper began to expand to small towns across the country. By the time Grit celebrated its 50th year in 1932, circulation was up to 400,000.

Grit is one of the longest-running publications in the country and has been a part of the American tapestry, particularly in the Heartland and rural areas throughout the nation, for many, many years.

What has made Grit such a success is the *Good News* it contains. The news you read in Grit will bring a smile to your face. A steady diet of the NY Times, CNN, and Fox, not to mention the crazy Facebook and Twitter posts that are bombarding all of us today, can actually put you into depression.

The Lord's plan for us, according to Jeremiah 29:11, is to give us a future and a hope. His plans are always for good. Jesus said that He came to bring us "life and life more abundantly" (John 10:10).

If you've been feeling as though the world is going to Hell in a hand-basket, maybe you've been reading the wrong newspaper. Actually, the future is bright and optimistic for those who are looking at the Lord. Each day is a new adventure and an opportunity to know Him better.

True happiness can be found in the pages of the Bible. A computer analysis of the Bible has determined that Psalm 103:1-2 are the center verses of the Bible. This is derived from the King James Version which has an even number of verses (31,102).

Using this computation, the middle verses read as follows: "Bless the LORD, O my soul: and all that is within me; bless his holy name. Bless the LORD, O my soul, and forget not all his benefits" (Ps. 103:1). I choose to bless the Lord. How about you?

SCRIPTURES FOR MEDITATION
(Selah – think on these things)

MONDAY: *I am so grateful that my future is in God's hands.*

Scriptures: Job 23:10, 42:10-13; Psalm 73:23-26; Jeremiah 29:11-14; Matthew 24:35; Revelation 21:1-5.

TUESDAY: *I will do my best to share the REAL 'Good News' today!*

Scripture: Psalm 68:11; Matthew 28:18-20; Acts 8:4-8, 26-38, 17:2-6; Romans 1:16; I Corinthians 15:1-4.

WEDNESDAY: *I will not be shaken by current events for my eyes are on the Lord.*

Scriptures: 2 Kings 6:15-17, 19:14-19, 32-37; Psalm 46:1-3; Lamentations 3:21-24; Acts 27:22-25.

THURSDAY: *I will live a thankful life.*

Scriptures: Psalm 100:1-5, 103:1-5; Jonah 2:9; Luke 17:12-19; Philippians 4:6-7; I Thessalonians 5:18.

FRIDAY: *Every day I will bless the Lord. His praises SHALL be in my mouth.*

Scriptures: Genesis 24:27; Deuteronomy 8:7-10; Judges 5:9; 2 Samuel 22:47-51; I Chronicles 16:36.

SATURDAY: *I will be careful what my eyes gaze upon, knowing the lust of the eyes can cause one to slip away from God.*

Scriptures: Genesis 13:6-18; Job 31:1; Psalm 101:3, 121:1-2; Proverbs 23:26; Matthew 6:22-23.

Week 27

GOD'S 800 NUMBER

A dozen or so years ago, while driving to Jekyll Island to attend a ladies' retreat, I made a few last-minute calls from my car phone to finalize some real estate transactions. As I traveled, I noticed I wasn't the only driver holding the steering wheel with one hand and a phone in the other.

Back then, when we had car phones instead of cell phones, it was quite common to see people, ranging from teenagers in their jazzed-up sports cars to the older generation like myself, busily engaged in conversations as they were driving along.

I'll never forget my first experience with a car phone. My brother, who at that time was a building contractor, was conducting important business over his phone as we drove through the beautiful Sierra mountain range. I was fascinated with the convenience, as well as the business possibilities of having a phone at one's finger tips while driving. What a time saver! (This is totally against the law now in California and in many other states!)

Completing his umpteenth call, he handed me the phone and said, "Go ahead Jerri. Call someone." I was as excited as a schoolgirl, as I dialed my honey back in Georgia.

"What?" You're in Doug's car?" Charlie asked in surprise.

"Isn't this neat?" I asked. "We're up in the mountains, not a building in sight. I've got to get one of these when I get back home."

Infatuated by this futuristic technology, after talking to Charlie I called a few other friends and family members. "Mom, you're crazy," laughed Sandy from her post at the nurse's station in the hospital. "This is probably costing Uncle Doug a fortune." OOPS! Sorry Doug.

It wasn't long after my return to Georgia that I, along with all my children, equipped our cars with phones; cellular phones, pagers, fax machines and now . . . e-mail. What next? You might say we're a "connected family."

Zipping along Hwy 341 to Jekyll Island I began to reminisce about the excitement I felt while using Doug's car phone that first time; realizing I could have a conversation from my car in the mountains of California all the way to a person in Georgia, simply amazed me.

Figure 40 - God's 800 Number

No confines, just the beauty of the snowcapped mountains to enjoy while talking cross country with the ones I loved. I suddenly realized how this type of communication has become "old hat." Now the car phone, once a wonder, has evolved into a cell phone to become just another way to keep in touch.

That's the way with most things in life . . . whether it's that first shiny, new car, the first piece of new furniture for your beginner apartment, or your first computer. Things become commonplace and ordinary . . . mere infatuations. Even Solomon, the richest potentate of his day, lamented he had accumulated everything that could be had, tried every new invention of his day, and yet it was all vanity . . . empty baubles apart from God.

Can it happen in the spiritual realm? Can the things of God become commonplace . . . ordinary . . . unexciting? Unfortunately, the answer all too often is yes!

Remember when your first met Christ? Wow! You felt so clean . . . so new. All the burden of sin was gone and in its place, was the first-time awareness that an eternal world actually existed? And God? He was so real. Not a day, not a moment that you were not aware He was with you? The Bible? You devoured its pages. You lugged it with you everywhere you went. Who cared if you looked like a religious nut? God's Word was sweeter than honey. And church? Oh my, you were there every time the door opened.

Then . . . slowly, but surely, that warm, comfortable fire in your heart started to cool . . . prayer became a chore and bible reading was reduced to a few hasty chapters now and then. You started taking your relationship with the Lord for granted. Church attendance became an on again, off again happening. Sunday nights? Definitely out . . . too many good programs on TV in that time slot. Sorry God.

Suddenly you notice something . . . a lot of static on the phone . . . batteries obviously in need of charging. The pager doesn't seem to buzz anymore, and the computer screen is blank. Calls to IBM's support number or the Geek Squad aren't returned. Communication is nearly gone. You're in trouble.

How could this happen?

Friend, if this is your story I have Good News for you. God has an 800 number. It's called P. R. A. Y. E. R. Call Him today. Get that excitement and love for Him back in your life. I can assure you His line is never busy. He won't put you on hold. There won't be a computerized voice telling you to punch in another number. He'll be there.

"Call upon me and I will answer thee and show thee great and mighty things which thou knowest not" (Jeremiah 33:3).

SCRIPTURES FOR MEDITATION
(Selah – think on these things)

MONDAY: *I will not take my relationship with the Lord for granted.*

Scriptures: Judges 10:10-16, 16:18-21; 2 Samuel 11:1-5, 26-27, 12:7-10; Psalm 51:1-12.

TUESDAY: *I will make my time with God a priority.*

Scripture: Deuteronomy 26:10; Psalm 16:8, 63:1-2; Proverbs 8:17; Isaiah 26:9; Matthew 6:33, 14:23-24.

WEDNESDAY: *I will not look to man for help for the Lord IS my helper!*

Scriptures: I Samuel 7:12; 2 Chronicles 14:11-12; Psalm 30:10, 40:17; Hebrews 13:6.

THURSDAY: *I will be on guard against drifting away from God.*

Scriptures: Proverbs 4:10-18; 2 Corinthians 6:14-18; Ephesians 6:10-18; Hebrews 2:1-3.

FRIDAY: *I will return to my first love and not allow myself to become lukewarm.*

Scriptures: Luke 9:62, 14:16-24, 15:11-24; John 6:66-71; James 5:20; Revelation 3:14-16.

SATURDAY: *I am so thankful that God is never too busy to listen to me.*

Scriptures: Genesis 21:14-21; Exodus 3:7-9; I Samuel 1:9-20; Isaiah 65:24; Jeremiah 33:1-3.

Week 28
LET US PRAY

"I saw people falling . . . and blood. I told him to be calm, drop the gun. He just kind of slouched down and dropped the gun." (Ben Strong)

When the shooting spree was over three young people were dead and five were wounded. This didn't happen on the streets of Chicago, or in the ghettoes of New York, but at a prayer meeting!

When many of us were pondering where we would find the best Christmas sales, December 1, 1997 was becoming indelibly imprinted on the minds of thirty-five high school students in West Paducah, Kentucky.

A fourteen-year-old freshman, identified by his peers as Michael Carneal, is alleged to have opened fire with a stolen pistol, on students who had gathered for their daily prayer meeting. The day after the shooting 200 students crowded into the prayer room. Ben Strong, the courageous young man who had persuaded Carneal to drop his weapon, led his classmates, and most of the faculty, in prayer.

Carneal had warned Strong, a minister's son and president of the prayer group, to stay away from Monday's prayer meeting. Although Strong was worried, he never expected to see the blood bath that would take place. He was a committed Christian who had endured the taunts from the self-proclaimed atheists on the campus. Like his Christian brothers and sisters, he would let nothing stop him from keeping his appointment with his friends for prayer. They had fought long and hard to get this privilege back and they were not retreating.

The lawsuit to stop Bible recitations and prayer in public schools was started by the Madalyn Murray O'Hair family back in 1959. (O'Hair died 2 years prior to this shooting.) By the sixties, displaying a bible in public schools was prohibited; even a bible placed on a desk in a public school became a criminal offense.

Fred Randolph, a personal friend and now a retired school teacher living in Hawkinsville, GA, experienced firsthand the consequences of taking a bible to school. While teaching in a public school in the Northeastern section of our country, Randolph lost his job because of his refusal to take his bible off his desk.

Several years ago, at a revival meeting in our church, a young evangelist shared about the early Christians who died as martyrs. This especially intrigued me since I had visited the grave site of one of the church's earliest martyrs in Southern India.

St. Thomas is reported to have established seven churches in that area. Around 68 A.D., while in a cave praying and pleading with God for the souls of the Indian people Thomas, one of the twelve original apostles, had a spear thrust in his side. I was humbled by this visit. What hardship and dedication, to leave Jerusalem and go to the jungles of India to spread the Gospel! I *thought* my mission trip to India was an act of faith. My travel in the air-conditioned comfort of a jet was a far cry from what Thomas endured on his journey.

The classic, Fox's Book of Martyrs, is replete with stories of real life heroes, who gave all because of their belief in a resurrected Christ. Ignatius was devoured by wild beasts; Alexander beheaded; Rhais had boiled pitch poured upon her head; Hippolytus was tied to a wild horse and dragged until he expired. In the most unimaginable ways, millions of Christians have died for their faith. Under the city of Rome are some six hundred miles of catacombs. Like berths on a ship, the graves of Christians are stacked, one above another.

What about today? Are Christians still suffering for Christ? According to the latest statistics, 20 million Christians were killed for their faith in the 20th Century. In the 21st Century, according to one credible report, worldwide more than 100,000 Christians are being killed each year.

But that's *"over there."*

Really?

Ask the parents of 15-year-old Kayce Steger, 17-year-old Jessica James and 14-year-old Nichole Hadley. Their kids used to live in Kentucky . . . until they attended a prayer meeting.

Could it happen in your town? Would you still go to a prayer meeting if you had just witnessed a killing in that location? In Paducah, Kentucky, one day after the slaughter had taken place, 200 kids did. For sure the devil didn't win that round . . . he just added fuel to a fire for God that was already burning. And the fire continues to grow.

Figure 41 – Monument to Slain Kids

Shortly after the massacre on December 5th, CNN televised the funeral of the slain teenagers. At the request of the grieving parents, Steven Curtis Chapman, a nationally known Christian singer, gave the Gospel message and extended an invitation to receive Jesus Christ as personal Savior. Quite possibly millions of people heard the Gospel for the first time.

Pray that violence in our public schools will be stopped. Pray that young people will turn their hearts to Christ. Pray for Christian young people to take a bold stand for what they believe in.

Let us (all) pray!

"They were stoned, they were sawn asunder, were tempted, were slain with the sword . . . of whom the world was not worthy . . ." (Hebrews 11:37- 38).

SCRIPTURES FOR MEDITATION

(Selah – think on these things)

MONDAY: *I will boldly take my stand for Christ everywhere I go!*

Scriptures: Proverbs 28:1; Acts 4:12-20, 5:25-33, 8:1-8; Romans 8:31-19; Philippians 1:14-20.

TUESDAY: *I will remember those who stood for God in Bible times as well as in modern times.*

Scripture: I Kings 18:20-22, 37-40; Jeremiah 38:1-13; Daniel 1:8, 6:7-23; Hebrews 11:32-38.

WEDNESDAY: *I will remember that our battle is not against flesh and blood, but against the deceiver, Satan.*

Scriptures: Isaiah 14:12-17; Matthew 4:1-11; Mark 8:32-33; Luke 13:11-16; Ephesians 6:12.

THURSDAY: *I have confidence that God will take that which seems bad and turn it into good.*

Scriptures: Genesis 50:18-20; 2 Kings 5:1-3, 13-15; Daniel 3:16-25; Luke 24:13-32; Acts 16:22-28.

FRIDAY: *I will support through prayer and giving those who are taking the battle to the front lines for God.*

Scriptures: Matthew 6:6; Acts 12:5-7; Philippians 4:6-10; Colossians 2:2-4; Hebrews 6:10.

SATURDAY: *I will remember that suffering for Christ is an honor.*

Scriptures: Luke 9:57-62; 2 Corinthians 11:23-31; Philippians 1:20-24; I Peter 3:13-18, 4:12-16, 5:7-11.

Week 29

THE BLESSINGS CONTINUE

I remember walking out of the doctor's office with a very discouraged husband. Although the diagnosis was nothing major, it met the criteria for another surgery. This time it was his shoulder.

Shoulder surgery recovery is tough, but when you throw in problems in your back, knee, and sugar levels, it's enough to get you down . . . if you let it. Charlie and I determined to major on our blessings instead.

As we drove back to Cochran we reminded ourselves of the many physical and spiritual blessings we both enjoy. On the physical side, we're still in our right minds, not confined to a nursing home or wheelchair; no cancer or other dread disease.

All our five senses are still working (although one missing hearing aid reduces that blessing a little) and our sense of humor is growing in our old age, rather than diminishing. Our conclusion: we're in great shape for the condition we're in.

Add to those blessings the blessing of living in this great country! As we waited for the doctor I looked at the wall and read the following prayer:

"Dear Lord, Thou great Physician, I kneel before Thee since every good and perfect gift must come from Thee. I pray: Give skill to my hand, good clear vision to my mind, kindness, and sympathy to my heart.

"Give me singleness of purpose, strength to lift at least a part of the burden of my suffering fellowmen. And a true realization of the privilege that is mine. Take from my heart, all guile and worldliness, that with the simple faith of a child, I may rely on Thee. In the Name of Jesus, Amen."

Having traveled behind the Bamboo Curtain and met with the Underground Church, I realized what a great blessing this little plaque proclaims. We are blessed to live in this country where a doctor has the freedom to post a prayer on his office wall.

You won't find a publicly displayed prayer such as that in North Korea, Saudi Arabia, or Malaysia. If you even speak the name of Jesus in many countries you will be thrown in prison. When I was in China we had to substitute the word "brother" for Jesus and "bread" for the word *Bible*.

And here, in this wonderful country, we read the Bible publicly from the steps of our county courthouses, teach Bible studies in jails, detention centers and prisons and beam Christian radio and TV programming 24/7. Are we blessed or what?

Figure 42 - The Blessings Continue

We carry our Bibles not only into church, but into every public establishment that we care to do so. We are not intimidated into toning down our message, shutting down our churches or excuse our exuberance for God. We're free to post videos about our faith in the Lord Jesus Christ on Facebook and YouTube. Are we blessed or what?

The largest fellowship in the world is in Seoul, South Korea. Yoido Full Gospel Church is a Pentecostal church on Yoi Island. In 2007 they numbered one million members (and they only count tithing members!). They've dropped a little and now number around 800,000. Still, it's the largest Protestant Christian congregation in the world. (Maybe some quit tithing!)

Just a few miles to the north is The North Korean Communist regime that is determined to ban the exercise of freedom of religion the Yoido Full Gospel church enjoys. Recently North Korea tested an intercontinental ballistic missile that landed in the Sea of Japan. Our government is trying to pressure China into putting the squeeze on North Korea. Once again, we are on the brink of war and freedom is at stake.

Many of us still remember the Korean War. Charlie is a Korean veteran and the thought of history repeating itself in that region is not a pleasant thought for him.

We pray our president will have the courage to stand up against this ungodly regime and let them know that the American people value their freedom and the freedom of our South Korean Allies.

America is bone-weary of war. Our brave men and women in the military have been fighting and being killed or wounded in the Middle East since October 2001. This war is now the longest war in our country's 241-year history. We're tired, but determined to let freedom ring!

Patriots have lived and died so that Charlie's doctor has the freedom to hang a prayer in his office. Let us never take our freedoms for granted.

SCRIPTURES FOR MEDITATION
(Selah – think on these things)

MONDAY: *I will be grateful for my many blessings.*

Scriptures: Numbers 6:24-26; Deuteronomy 28:1-14; 2 Samuel 7:28-29; Psalm 84:12.

TUESDAY: *I am thankful for good health and a sound mind.*

Scripture: Psalm 103:1-3; Proverbs 4:20-22; Jeremiah 30:17; 2 Timothy 1:7; 3 John 1:2.

WEDNESDAY: *I know the Lord placed us in the exact time and place where we are so we can be a blessing to others.*

Scriptures: 2 Kings 4:8-17; Esther 4:14; Isaiah 6:1-8; Jeremiah 1:4-9; Acts 17:24-27, 20:35.

THURSDAY: *I am thankful the Lord is my Jehovah Rophe (The Lord my Healer) and whether He heals miraculously or through doctors and/or medicine I am thankful.*

Scriptures: Exodus 15:26; Isaiah 53:4-6; Mark 16:17-20; John 9:1-7, 24-25; I Peter 2:24.

FRIDAY: *Old age may appear to have drawbacks, but we will be thankful that every day with Jesus is sweeter than the day before!*

Scriptures: I Chronicles 29:26-28; Psalm 92:13-14; Proverbs 10:22, 16:31; Isaiah 46:3-4.

SATURDAY: *Even though wars may come and wars may go, I will remain confident that God will take care of me.*

Scriptures: Deuteronomy 33:6-7; Psalm 17:7-8, 91:1-10, 34:19; Matthew 24:4-8; Revelation 1:4-9.

Week 30
THE ULTIMATE RIP-OFF

In December 2008 Bernard (Bernie) Madoff was sent to jail to await sentencing after pleading guilty to eleven counts of fraud, money laundering, perjury and theft in New York's Manhattan Federal Court. Estimates of money bilked from Madoff's victims, was estimated to be around $70 billion. In June 2009, he was sentenced to 150 years in prison, the maximum allowed.

As Madoff stood facing the judge he said, "I cannot adequately express how sorry I am for what I have done. I am painfully aware that I have deeply hurt many, many people, including family, friends, and associates."

The apology was small compensation for those who lost their trusts, pension funds, hedge funds, retirements, and life savings: Madoff's elaborate scheme also wiped out many non-profit organizations. From his own clients, it was estimated that he cheated them out of nearly $18 billion. There are reports that at least two investors committed suicide. So much for a friendly working relationship with your stock broker!

The Wall Street Journal published a list of the thousands of organizations and individuals who lost money, among whom were TV host, Larry King; movie director, Steven Spielberg; and Nobel Prize winner and Holocaust survivor, Elie Wiesel. The Royal Bank of Scotland lost over L400 million. The number involved worldwide continued growing daily. No one will probably ever know the exact dollar amount.

Those who were ripped off experienced the gamut of emotions; utter sadness and despair; raging anger and the desire for revenge. This is only a partial list of feelings his clients experienced.

Former Gov. Mike Huckabee commented that he wished they would let Madoff out of jail, compel him to sell off his $7 million penthouse and all his goods; then live out of the garbage cans of New York. Others had stronger words.

Since we didn't invest in any of Madoff's companies or brokerage firms; Charlie and I weren't affected by his conniving schemes. However, I'm truly sorry for all the everyday, ordinary people who lost their life savings in the whole fiasco.

Can you even imagine what it would be like to wake up one morning and find that everything you have worked for your whole life has been for nothing? Try to imagine the disdain, disgust and abhorrence you would feel for the person responsible for doing this to you. They not only robbed you, but the people you loved as well.

No way would you want to even speak to such a person who cared so little for your well-being. One who cared only about his own pleasure and life style no matter the harm it would bring to you.

Figure 43 – Bernie Madoff

Someday there will be people who will wake up in a worse condition than Madoff's investors. These people have believed the greatest Ponzi scheme of all. They've listened to the deceiver of deceivers. His name is Satan and he has lied, connived and contrived to sell them down the river. He's made them think that this life is all there is. They've gathered riches and treasures, only to leave it all behind and wind up in Hell.

The Bible shares with us what they will say to Satan down in that place of the abyss . . . "down to Hell, to the sides of the pit. They that see him shall narrowly look upon him and consider him saying, 'Is this the man that made the earth to tremble, that did shake kingdoms?'" (Isaiah 14:12-17) He will be despised far more than Madoff or Hitler or Pharaoh of old.

Don't let the Devil rip you off. Turn your life over to the Lord Jesus Christ and you'll never suffer regrets. Invest in the Kingdom of God. The dividends are out of this world!

SCRIPTURES FOR MEDITATION

(Selah – think on these things)

MONDAY: *I will be mindful there is a judgment awaiting the lost, from which they will be damned for eternity.*

Scriptures: Ezekiel 3:17-21, 22:30, 33:7-9; Matthew 25:24-30; Luke 13:1-5; Revelation 20:11-15.

TUESDAY: *I will trust the Lord to lead me today to a lost person to warn them of the judgment to come.*

Scripture: Proverbs 11:30; Jeremiah 1:6-9; Daniel 12:2-3; John 1:40-42, 4:24-29; Hebrews 10:26-27.

WEDNESDAY: *I will be aware there is no place to hide from God. Our God is omnipresent.*

Scriptures: 2 Chronicles 16:9; Psalm 139:1-12; Proverbs 15:3; Jeremiah 23:24; John 1:48.

THURSDAY: *I believe God is extending His grace to all, regardless of their sin.*

Scriptures: 2 Chronicles 33:9-13; Luke 18:10-14; 1 Corinthians 1:26-29; 1 Timothy 1:12-17; 2 Peter 3:9.

FRIDAY: *I will remember that serving God will reap dividends in the world to come.*

Scriptures: Matthew 6:19-21; Mark 9:41, 12:41-44; 2 Corinthians 4:16-18; 2 Timothy 4:6-8.

SATURDAY: *I will pray for those who are incarcerated, remembering there is still hope for anyone if they will turn to Jesus.*

Scriptures: Jeremiah 33:3; Matthew 25:34-36; I Thessalonians 5:17; Philemon 1:10-18; James 5:16.

Week 31
DONORS NEEDED

Some time ago we drove past a church sign that read, "Be an organ donor. Give your heart to Jesus." What a terrific thought. Charlie was so challenged by the mini-message he shared it with the inmates at the Dooly State Prison, where we teach a monthly Bible study. He told the inmates that each one of them could be an organ donor.

It's true we can all be organ donors in a spiritual sense, yet there are many people who literally hover between life and death, waiting for physical organ transplants.

The Discovery Health Channel ran a six-part series of one-hour episodes entitled, GIFT OF LIFE. Each episode followed donor families, transplant coordinators, and recipients through the complex web of logistics, surgery, and emotion involved in the world of organ procurement and transplantation.

Each day about 70 people receive an organ transplant, but another 16 people on the waiting list die, because not enough organs are available.

Chris Klug became a bronze medalist in 2002 at the Salt Lake City Winter Olympics. "You might think the best day of my life was the day I won the Olympic medal, but the most beautiful day was when someone decided to be an organ donor and saved my life," said Chris at a Coalition on Donation.

Sharing about his life before the transplant operation, Chris stated that waiting was the hardest part. "I wore a pager every minute of the day and carried a cell phone as a backup in anticipation of receiving a call from the University Hospital transplant team informing me that a liver was available that matched my blood type."

Nine years earlier, Chris was diagnosed with PSC (Primary Sclerosing Cholangitis), a rare, degenerative liver condition. Without a transplant Chris would have died.

Randall Barron, a dear friend of ours, was a retired pharmacist who, after retirement, became an enthusiastic promoter for organ donations. Randall received a new liver in the nineties and personally knew what it meant to be an organ recipient. Before his death he traveled extensively throughout the southwest sharing his experience as a transplant recipient at Rotary Clubs. Randall enjoyed an extra 17.5 years of life because of his transplant.

Charlie's cousin, Dorma Westlotorn, received a liver transplant nearly 30 years ago! Today at age 87 she is still in the *go* mode and planning a big hurrah for her next birthday. You really have to be a *goer* to keep up with cousin Dorma!

The latest statistics in 2017 show there are nearly

Figure 44 – Charlie & Cousin Dorma Westlotorn

118,000 people on the official waiting list for organ transplants, and thousands need tissue and corneal transplants each year. This year nearly 173,000 people will be diagnosed with a blood disease called "leukemia." Many could possibly be cured by transplant procedures. The chance to live a full life won't come unless many more of us consider organ and tissue donation.

Transplantation saves lives, but only if we help. All we need to do is say *yes* to organ and tissue donation on our donor card and/or driver's license, sign up on our state's donor registry and discuss our decision with our family. Even if we've given signed permission, our family may be asked to give consent before donation can occur.

Hopefully no one else in my family will ever need an organ transplant. Right now, everyone looks healthy and hearty, but life is fragile. There are no guarantees. Somewhere, someone needs help today . . . maybe someone close to you. Will you give the gift of life and sign up as an organ donor?

And, by all means, plan to be a spiritual donor and give your heart to Jesus. Remember, He gave His all for you! "For God so loved the world, He gave His only begotten son, that whosoever believeth in Him, should not perish, but have everlasting life" (John 3:16).

SCRIPTURES FOR MEDITATION

(Selah – think on these things)

MONDAY: *My organs can be shared after I die, but while I'm alive I can personally share eternal life with others.*

Scriptures: Psalm 40:1-3; Mark 5:18-19; Acts 5:42, 8:3-6; 16:14-15, 20:20-21.

TUESDAY: *Just as Randall felt a personal responsibility to share with others about life saving transplants, so I should feel a personal responsibility to share Christ with others.*

Scripture: 2 Kings 7:3-9; Luke 19:1-10; Acts 9:13-16; Romans 1:14-16; Galatians 1:15-24.

WEDNESDAY: *I need to be grateful for the blessings God gives me every day, instead of bemoaning the 'things' I don't have.*

Scriptures: Romans 7:7; Philippians 4:11-13; Colossians 3:1-5; 1Timothy 6:6-8; Hebrews 13:5-6.

THURSDAY: *If an organ recipient feels gratitude toward his or her donor, what should my attitude be toward the Lord who gave up His life for me?*

Scriptures: Matthew 26:6-13; Luke 7:37-48; Philippians 2:5-11; Revelation 4:10-11.

FRIDAY: *I will remember that life is fragile and each day is a gift from God.*

Scriptures: Psalm 90:10, 118:24; Proverbs 27:1; Lamentations 3:22-23; Luke 12:16-21.

SATURDAY: *I will do my best to be more thoughtful when I hear of families who have lost loved ones, knowing our family could be next.*

Scriptures: Genesis 47:27-31; John 11:35; Romans 12:15; 2 Corinthians 1:3-6; Hebrews 9:27.

Week 32
MYSTERY HOUSE

Because of the incredible heat wave this summer, I couldn't help noticing the lush, green lawn in front of the gutted brick house located south of Macon. Nestled in the trees, the remains of the obviously uninhabitable building have been meticulously cared for throughout the years. What happened to this brick shell that was once a home? Why was someone taking care of it as if it were a residence? Was it a shrine to someone who possibly lost their life in a tragic fire? It was a mystery.

Over the years, as I've traveled back and forth from Cochran to Macon, I've noticed subtle changes. Several times the brick shell has been repainted, on occasion the lawn furniture has been moved; but always the grass is neatly mowed, shrubs carefully trimmed, and in the heat of summer the sprinklers are on. I've heard stories that would seemingly support the "shrine" theory; but there has never been anyone around at the times I happen to pass by that could confirm those stories.

One day a friend mentioned the house to me and we expressed to each other our mutual curiosity as to what had happened there. "Jerri," she challenged, "you need to see if you can find out 'who and why' someone is keeping everything painted and cared for." She too, had heard that it might possibly be kept up as a shrine to a loved one. My curiosity was growing. I had to solve the mystery. (Some might call this being nosey.)

"Honey, when I turn off the interstate today, if someone's at that house, I'm going to stop!" Charlie just shook his head. (Men . . . they just don't understand a woman's curiosity!)

"Okay," he sighed, secretly hoping I would forget this whole mystery business. Since my friend and I had discussed the house, I had pointed it out to Charlie, mentioning the possibility of a murder . . . or suicide . . . or?

As we turned on Sgoda Road, I was delighted to see an older, white-haired lady watering the shrubbery. "Look!" I exclaimed ecstatically. "Someone's actually there."

The owner graciously recounted the events surrounding the fateful day of the fire. Aware that many tales had circulated in the community as to what had happened, she was more than happy to explain the mystery to me. I must confess I was a little disappointed with the actual account. None of my theories were correct. No deep, dark secret had been hidden.

The owner told us that on Christmas Day in 1975, around four o'clock in the afternoon, a fire gutted her home. The only deaths that had occurred were those of her two little dogs. The fire department had checked for arson, but discarded that idea and ruled the fire had started in the furnace. As to the reason she was taking care of the house and grounds? In her words, "I just can't decide how to rebuild."

As we drove off, headed south to Cochran on Highway 87, we just shook our heads. "Can't decide how to rebuild?" I repeated again. "Incredible!"

Figure 45 - Mystery House

Now, when I pass the mystery house, I've decided it's a greater mystery than ever! Why would anyone continue to keep up the exterior of a house, year after year, with nothing on the inside? You can't live in this house. Oh, sure . . . the paint always looks fresh, the yard is always mowed and people even come by to visit. (There's a bench to the left of the house where the owner sits at times, visiting with her friends and relatives.)

The clock is ticking for all of us. Will the owner of the house on Sgoda Road ever make that decision to rebuild her house? Will she ever be able to enjoy a winter evening on the inside of her home, or will she only have a shell to admire and care for during the remainder of her days?

How many people do you know that keep up the outside appearances but there's nothing on the inside? Oh, they know they need to make a decision about their house. People have talked with them about receiving Christ, but they just can't decide whether to invite Him in and make their shell a place of God's habitation. Their indecision is keeping them from the joy of Christ's fellowship on the inside!

What about you friend? Is everything on the exterior looking good, but nothing is on the inside? Your clothes look great, your makeup is perfect, your hair is always in place . . . but are you empty?

Indecision . . . now that's a mystery! Why would anyone procrastinate in making the most important decision of their lives? Don't delay in making your decision to receive Christ. He will fill all the empty places and give your life purpose and meaning. You were created by Him and for Him. He gives you the right to make this decision and will not force His way into your shell.

Solve your own mystery friend. Do it today!

"Behold, I stand at the door and knock: if any man hear my voice, and open the door, I will come in to him, and will sup with him, and he with me" (Revelation 3:20).

SCRIPTURES FOR MEDITATION
(Selah – think on these things)

MONDAY: *I am so glad God gave us a free will to choose Him.*

Scriptures: Deuteronomy 30:15-20; Joshua 24:21-24; 1 Kings 18:21; Joel 3:14; John 6:66-69; Revelation 22:17.

TUESDAY: *I will diligently seek to know God better today than I knew Him yesterday.*

Scripture: Psalm 143:6-8; Proverbs 25:2; Isaiah 55:6; Hosea 6:3; 2 Corinthians 8:7; 1Peter 1:4-7.

WEDNESDAY: *I am so glad the Word of God reveals many mysteries to His children.*

Scriptures: Mark 4:10-12; Romans 11:21-25, 16:25-27; 1 Corinthians 2:6-8; Ephesians 1:7-12.

THURSDAY: *I will be content to know there are some things we are not supposed to know. God has a purpose in not revealing everything to us.*

Scriptures: Deuteronomy 29:29; Isaiah 64:4; Matthew 24:32-36; Mark 13:31-37; Acts 1:6-7.

FRIDAY: *I will not be a procrastinator when it comes to the things of God.*

Scriptures: Proverbs 27:1, 31:27-31; Ecclesiastes 10:18; Matthew 25:1-13; James 4:14-17.

SATURDAY: *I will be more focused on what condition my heart is in, rather than what I look like on the outside.*

Scriptures: Psalm 51:10; Proverbs 4:23; Jeremiah 17:9-10, 29:13; Matthew 22:37-38; 1 Peter 3:3-4.

Week 33
NO GREATER LOVE

John Daniel's last memory of his friend and comrade Richard Etchberger, was of him being hoisted up into a helicopter by Etchberger. Shot in both legs, Daniel passed out and when he woke up at Udorn Air Base in Thailand he learned that his friend had died saving his life.

Ever since that day Daniel has wondered why he lived and not his friend. "Every day I think about it and I'm grateful for what Dick did for me," he says.

According to military reports, "On 11 March 1968, Chief Master Sergeant Richard L. Etchberger was manning a defensive position when the base in Laos was overrun by an enemy ground force. With his entire crew dead or wounded, Chief Etchberger continued to return the enemy's fire; thus, denying it access to the position.

"During this entire period, Chief Etchberger continued to direct air strikes and call for air rescue on his emergency radio, thereby enabling the air evacuation force to locate the surrounded friendly element. When air rescue arrived, Chief Etchberger deliberately exposed himself to enemy fire in order to place his three surviving wounded comrades in the rescue slings permitting them to be airlifted to safety.

"As Chief Etchberger was finally being rescued, he was fatally wounded, by enemy ground fire. His fierce defense, which culminated in the sacrifice of his life, saved not only the lives of his three comrades but provided for the successful evacuation of the remaining survivors of the base."

The entire operation had taken place in Laos during the Vietnam War. Laos was a neutral country and our troops were not supposed to be there. When Etchberger died his family was simply told that he died in a helicopter crash. The classified information was not released for nearly two decades.

Richard Loy Etchberger, a non-commissioned officer in the United States Air Force and was posthumously awarded the United States military's highest decoration, the Medal of

Honor, for his actions during the Battle of Lima site 85 in the Vietnam War.

The medal was formally presented to his three sons by former President Barack Obama during a ceremony at the White House on September 21, 2010.

John Daniel, now 78, was also at the ceremony. Today he lives in a small town in Colorado with his wife. He has children, grandchildren and two great-grandchildren.

Daniel says he thinks back often to his last moments with Dick Etchberger. "I said 'Dick, Dick, we're not going to get out of here!' and he says, 'I know, say your last prayers, that's all you can do.'"

Today, Daniel prays for the wisdom to make good on a debt he can never repay. "It has to be that God is not done with me on the face of the earth yet. Thanks to Dick Etchberger, I'm still alive to do something," he said.

Figure 46 - No Greater Love

As I watched the touching Medal of Honor ceremony on TV, I thought long and hard about Daniel's comments. Every day he thinks about his friend's sacrifice. He said that he was grateful every day for the sacrifice made on his behalf and I wondered . . . Am I grateful every day for the sacrifice Jesus Christ made for me on the cross?

Daniel told reporters, "I have one grandchild to carry on my status. He's in the Air Force, on active duty." A framed photo of Daniel's grandson, Airman 1st Class Jerry W. Daniel, sits on a shelf in his living room. Next to the picture is a painting depicting Daniel being hoisted into the helicopter as Etchberger looks on. The painting is an artist's rendering of Daniel's last memory of Etchberger.

Daniel said he knows that if not for the bravery of Etchberger 49 years ago, it could easily be someone else sitting in his living room, living out his life. "I don't know why me, but it is," he said. "And Dick's presence is in my life every day."

Etchberger died on the floor of the chopper as it headed off to safety. Jesus died on a cross. "Greater love hath no man than this; that a man lay down his life for his friends" (John 15:13).

As a post script on this story, Daniel and the two other men who were saved by Etchberger's sacrifice were recently interviewed for an upcoming TV special for the next Medal of Honor Day to be held in March 2018.

SCRIPTURES FOR MEDITATION

(Selah – think on these things)

MONDAY: *I am so grateful for our veterans. I will hold them up today in my prayers.*

Scriptures: 1 Samuel 12:23; Nehemiah 4:6-9; 1 Thessalonians 5:17; 1 Timothy 2:1-8; 1 Peter 2:17.

TUESDAY: *I will live thankfully today knowing military men and women are protecting our country and I will trust God to protect them!*

Scripture: 2 Chronicles 32:20-22; Psalm 33:12, 91:1-7; Proverbs 29:2; Daniel 6:22; John 15:13-14.

WEDNESDAY: *I believe there is a reason God has allowed me to live until this very day and I will do my best to honor Him with all my remaining days.*

Scriptures: Deuteronomy 33:25; I Samuel 2:30; Psalm 34:1-3, 139:23-24; Proverbs 20:6.

THURSDAY: *I resolve to be a good example to others, even as Chief Etchberger displayed such a selfless act of courage in dying for his men.*

Scriptures: Matthew 16:24-26; Mark 8:35-36; 1 Corinthians 11:1; 1 Thessalonians 2:12-14.

FRIDAY: *I will not do deeds of kindness for selfish reasons and personal glory. I will remember that God sees what I am doing and also sees my motives.*

Scriptures: Proverbs 21:14; Jeremiah 17:9-10; Matthew 6:1-6; Acts 5:1-11; Hebrews 4:9-13.

SATURDAY: *I'm sure Chief Etchberger's sons were very proud of their father when the President presented them with his posthumous Medal of Honor. Lord, help me to so live that my children will be proud of me.*

Scriptures: Genesis 18:17-19; Psalm 128:1-6; Proverbs 10:7, 22:1, 31:28; Revelation 14:13.

Week 34
PLAYING CUPID

A few years ago, during one of Charlie's orthopedic appointments, his surgeon told us the sweetest story about a couple of his patients. The people, both in their '90s, confirmed my suspicions about romance: It's not your age that matters; it's your state of mind.

The doctor said that Mr. Jones (as I'll call him) was having some orthopedic work done and the good doctor stopped by his room on his morning rounds.

The old boy was chipper as usual and the doctor, knowing he was a widower, asked him a couple of questions just for fun.

"Mr. Jones," began the doctor, "what would you like in a woman if you decided to get married again?"

The ninety-three-year-old responded quickly and said, "She would have to be able to cook and drive."

That made a lot of sense to the good doctor and so he left Mr. Jones' room and stopped to see his next patient. Ms. Kilgore (not her real name), a widow of some years, had bounced back from her surgery amazingly well for a ninety-two-year-old.

All of a sudden, the doctor had an idea. "Ms. Kilgore," he asked with a knowing twinkle in his eye. "Can you cook?"

"Can I cook?" she said with indignation. "I sure can. I still cook for my whole family."

This was going better than the doctor could imagine. "Can you drive?" Again, the answer was in the affirmative and the doctor began to put his plan into action.

"There's a man I want you to meet in the room next door." The doctor laughed and laughed as he relayed this story to Charlie and me. "The next time I saw them they were walking down the hallway together."

We could tell the doctor was pleased with himself at playing cupid. It will be interesting when we see the doctor again to find out if his arrows have really hit their mark with Mr. Jones and Ms. Kilgore.

Some people today may need a little help in meeting their mates. I'm amazed at how many people are meeting online through organizations promising everything from true love to matches made in Heaven.

Even Christian organizations (think: Christianmingle.com) are getting into the cyber romance market; doing their best to bring Christian men and women together in hopes of lonely people finding happiness through wedded bliss.

Figure 47 – Wade & Bonnie Conklin

One Bible account tells of Abraham sending his servant to a faraway country in search of a proper bride for his beloved son, Isaac. She had to be of a certain family and have strength of character and a heart to serve. The search and the fulfillment of the servant's prayer are beautifully portrayed in Genesis 24.

I can't speak for anyone else, but I'm glad that I left the choosing of my mate up to God. The Holy Spirit can bring the perfect mate along when we put our trust in Him. "Seek ye first the kingdom of God and His righteousness and all these things will be added unto you" (Matthew 6:33).

The Bible says, "Be anxious for nothing, but by prayer and supplication let your requests be made known unto God and the peace of God that passeth understanding will keep your hearts and minds through Christ Jesus" (Philippians 4:6-7).

And by the way, I'm certainly not opposed to bringing two strangers together as the good doctor did. A couple of our dearest friends, Bonnie and Wade Conklin, were brought together on a blind date and they feel that God had His hand in that meeting in a big way. They have now been married for eight years and are faithfully serving the Lord and bringing blessing to so many lives.

Whether you're in your twenties or in your nineties, let God be your cupid. He can put things together in the neatest ways, even if He has to use an orthopedic surgeon to do it.

"Trust in the Lord with all thine heart and lean not unto thine own understanding. In all thy ways acknowledge Him and He will direct thy paths" (Proverbs 3:5-6).

SCRIPTURES FOR MEDITATION

(Selah – think on these things)

MONDAY: *I love the fact that God designed the first home when He created man AND woman and placed them in the Garden of Eden.*

Scriptures: Genesis 2:20-25, 24:1-9, 63-67; Matthew 19:3-11; Mark 10:7-9; Ephesians 5:20-32.

TUESDAY: *I will remember that waiting on God is not a waste of time.*

Scripture: Psalm 27:13-14, 37:3-7; Isaiah 40:28-31; Matthew 6:27-33; Philippians 1:9-10.

WEDNESDAY: *I will remember that every encounter with*

someone else could actually be one of God's Divine Appointments!

Scriptures: Ruth 2:1-6, 19-23; Luke 19:1-6, 24:13-32; John 4:6-10; Acts 8:27-40, 10:30-44.

THURSDAY: *I will remember that age is not a factor when it comes to hearing the Lord.*

Scriptures: Genesis 18:9-14; Deuteronomy 5:26-29; 1 Samuel 3:8-10; Psalm 92:12-15; Jeremiah 1:4-7.

FRIDAY: *I am thankful for a home founded on the Word of God. I will not take this blessing for granted.*

Scriptures: Joshua 24:14-15; Proverbs 12:7, 15:6; Matthew 7:24-27; 2 Timothy 1:1-5; Hebrews 11:7.

SATURDAY: *I can trust God for my future. Following His plan for my life is much better than my plan.*

Scriptures: Psalm 23:1-6; Jeremiah 29:11-14; 2 Corinthians 5:1-8; Philippians 3:13-14.

Week 35
WORDS TO LIVE BY

In 2006 former Vice-President Dick Cheney accidentally shot a companion during a weekend quail hunting trip in Texas. Fortunately, his hunting partner, Harry Whittington, only suffered minor wounds and survived the accident.

The shotgun pellets hit him in his cheek, neck and chest during the shooting incident. Whittington was looking in the tall grass for a bird he shot and had not warned Cheney and a third hunter of his location. When a covey was flushed, the Vice-President fired and Whittington went down.

Closer to home, another shotgun incident occurred that involved the son of one of our friends. Upon initial investigation, the shooting appeared to be an accident. The thirteen-year- old was shot in the head and died instantly. Law enforcement officials investigated the possibility of foul play at the hands of the fifteen-year-old involved in the tragic death. Subsequently it was ruled an accident.

When the father discovered the possibility of murder as opposed to an accident, the whole picture changed. Instead of feeling sorrow for the other child involved, emotions instantly changed to anger and disbelief.

Somehow, we can deal with accidents. We can make allowances for people if we feel that what they have done to us or someone we love has been unintentional. But deliberately shooting someone . . . or causing grief and anguish with evil intent, now that's another story.

An old saying goes: "Sticks and stones will break my bones, but words will never hurt me." How untrue is this little ditty, because words can do almost as much damage as the blast of a shotgun.

Marriages have been ripped apart, families torn asunder, churches split, and reputations ruined because of words. Communication is a powerful tool.

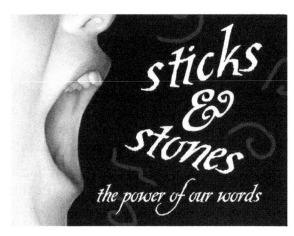

Figure 48 – Words Can Hurt

A few years back a group from our church went to Griffin, Georgia to attend a wonderful and inspiring couples retreat led by Dr. and Mrs. Mark Rutland. Dr. Rutland is president of Global Servants and was the third President of Oral Roberts University in Tulsa, Oklahoma.

Dr. Rutland wisely stated that men have two languages and women speak about twenty-eight! Just knowing what language we're speaking would really help our men to understand the female species.

Anyone that has been married, for even a short time, realizes the value of good communication skills in a successful union. One of the basic teachings put forth during the retreat was the importance of knowing the languages our mates are using.

All those attending the retreat seemed to go with sincere hearts to make their "good marriages better" (as the brochure stated). One of the most obvious faults in any marriage is the misuse of words. Words that tear down and demean our marriage partners can bring about division and eventual separation or even divorce. Words are powerful.

Making the deliberate choice to speak kind and edifying words over our mates and children can only enhance relationships. An accidental harsh word can be more easily overlooked and excused as opposed to cutting and biting words used to intentionally wound and cause damage.

Sometimes like Mr. Whittington, who was hidden in the pampas grass, we need to communicate where we are in our relationship. Likely, had he warned the VP of his location, he would not have been shot! The silent treatment really never helps anyone one understand where we're coming from.

Let our words be deliberately full of grace and love. Nothing will injure others more than thinking we have used words against them as weapons of mass destruction.

"Let no corrupt communication proceed out of your mouth but that which is good for the use of edifying, that it may minister grace unto the hearers" (Ephesians 4:29).

SCRIPTURES FOR MEDITATION

(Selah – think on these things)

MONDAY: *I will remember today the power of my words.*

Scriptures: Job 6:24; Psalm 139:4, 141:3; Proverbs 18:21; Mark 11:23; Ephesians 4:29.

TUESDAY: *Today I will ask God to give me boldness to speak His Word to others.*

Scripture: Nehemiah 8:1-8; Proverbs 28:1; Jeremiah 20:9; Acts 4:13-31; 2 Corinthians 7:1-4.

WEDNESDAY: *I will work to build good relationships with my family and friends.*

Scriptures: Ruth 3:10-11; Proverbs 14:1, 15:1-4, 18:24; Romans 12:10; 1 Corinthians 13:4-7; 1 Peter 3:1-9.

THURSDAY: *I will remember that words can build up or tear down.*

Scriptures: Genesis 37:3-4; Joshua 24:27; Proverbs 17:28, 25:11; Matthew 12:35-37.

FRIDAY: *I will remember that people are saved through "hearing" the Gospel. Lord, help me to speak Your Word to others.*

Scriptures: Isaiah 53:1; Matthew 28:19-20; Mark 16:15; Acts 5:19-20; Romans 8:10-15.

SATURDAY: *I am grateful for the Word of God that builds my faith each day.*

Scriptures: Psalm 19:7-11; Acts 20:32; Romans 10:17; Ephesians 6:17; Hebrews 4:12.

Week 36
THE LAST RESERVATION

What a great excuse for a fall vacation! Charlie's darling niece, Katie Estep was getting married in a beautiful resort area called Lake Lure in North Carolina. After canning umpteen jars of jams, peppers, and salsa, not to mention freezing peas, tomatoes, corn, and tons of blueberries; this old gal was ready for a much-needed vacation. How come no one told me how much work is involved in retirement?

We had known for some time about Katie's wedding and so when we received the invitation we began to make plans to travel to the Carolinas and enjoy the fall extravaganza of leaves. The Lord is very liberal with his brush when it comes to painting the fall colors in the eastern section of the United States. Charlie, being a native of West Virginia, grew up amid the beauty of this area.

Shortly after we received the invitation we were enjoying our morning coffee and began discussing the upcoming wedding. We talked about making our reservations, but the actual date of the wedding seemed a long way off to me. I told Charlie that I would get around to doing it sometime the following week.

Charlie thought otherwise and prodded me a little to go ahead and make our reservations. I looked up the number of the resort where Katie and Dillon were tying the knot and made the call.

What a surprise I got when I was told that I was getting the last reservation in the block of rooms reserved for the wedding guests! I can't begin to tell you how thrilled and relieved I was that Charlie had encouraged me to not procrastinate on getting our reservations secured.

Of course, we could have stayed in another hotel, or even in nearby Ashville for that matter, but being in the thick of things with family and friends would sure be a lot more fun.

Quite some time ago I made a reservation for another wedding that will be taking place in a location that is out of this world. The guest list is miles long and the reception will be attended by all those who are listed in the Who's Who of God's known and unknown people. You may know about some of the guests. Ever heard of Abraham, Isaac, and Jacob? How about Noah, Daniel, and Job?

Figure 49 – Dillon & Katie Kestner – Wedding Day

The groom is the Lord Jesus Christ himself, and everyone who has received Him as their Lord and Savior are part of His glorious bride. What a wedding that will be! I can't wait.

Unlike Katie and Dillon's wedding invitation, there is no date set for this wedding. The groom has told us to be ready at any time. He'll give a shout and we'll be on our way. There is one catch however; we need to make sure we have our reservation confirmed. When Jesus gives the shout to come up and meet him, it will be too late for those who have procrastinated in this most important detail.

Have you made your reservation? Are you ready or are you still procrastinating? "For the Lord Himself will descend from Heaven with a shout, with the voice of an archangel, and with the trumpet of God. And the dead in Christ will rise first. Then we who are alive and remain shall be caught up together with them in the clouds to meet the Lord in the air. And thus, we shall always be with the Lord" (I Thessalonians 4:16-17).

SCRIPTURES FOR MEDITATION

(Selah – think on these things)

MONDAY: *I am so glad the Lord extends His invitation for salvation to all!*

Scriptures: Matthew 11:28-30; John 3:16-18, 6:49-51; Acts 16:30-31; Romans 10:13.

TUESDAY: *I know that all men won't be saved, but I will do my best to extend the invitation to as many as I can to receive Christ.*

Scripture: Mark 1:14-18; Acts 8:2-8; Romans 1:14-16; 1 Corinthians 9:16-23.

WEDNESDAY: *Just as the bride prepares for her big day, so I must prepare for the day when my Heavenly Bridegroom calls me to Him.*

Scriptures: Isaiah 61:10; Matthew 25:1-13; 2 Corinthians 5:1-10; 1 John 5:6-10.

THURSDAY: *I am thankful that my name is written in the Lamb's Book of Life. I have made my reservation!*

Scriptures: Luke 10:19-20; Philippians 4:1-4; Revelation 3:5, 20:11-15, 21:25-27.

FRIDAY: *I am glad people can accept the Lord's invitation on their deathbed, but how much better to receive Him in their youth!*

Scriptures: Proverbs 27:1, 29:1; Ecclesiastes 12:1; Luke 23:39-43; 2 Timothy 3:14-17.

SATURDAY: *Every day down here on Earth is a dress rehearsal for what we will be doing in eternity. Help me Lord, to make my days count for You.*

Scriptures: Matthew 25:13-33; Luke 16:19-31; Galatians 6:7-10; 2 Timothy 4:6-8.

Week 37
MODERN DAY ESTHERS

Many years ago in Persia (now known as Iran) a Jewish queen stepped up to her destiny in defense of her people. A wicked man named Haman threatened the existence of her entire race.

Her uncle challenged her with words that have reverberated down through history: "For if you remain silent at this time, relief and deliverance for the Jews will arise from another place, but you and your father's family will perish. And who knows but that you have come to royal position for such a time as this?" (Esther 4:14)

In 2009 countless Iranian women stood up to the Haman of their time: Mahmoud Ahmadinejad. Graphic photos, of a young woman named Neda gripped the world. She was shot in the chest in cold blood as she stood next to her father. She is now honored as a martyr.

Figure 50 – Martyr – Neda Agha-Soltan

Those of us who are old enough to remember the Iranian revolt against the Shah in 1979 were shocked to see women wielding rocks and standing at the forefront of the thousands of protestors demanding freedom from the Haman-like dictator.

As images of events were relayed by cell phones to the media and by the Internet through Twitter, Myspace, and Facebook; we saw prophecy being fulfilled before our eyes. Today, the world is crying for a leader who will bring peace. The stage is being set for the Antichrist.

Jesus spoke of these end times when there would be distress of nations. Ezekiel the prophet foretold of a major war in the Middle East, and named the nations that would be aligned together. Where is Iran in all of this? According to Scripture Iran is lined up with ancient Cush, Libya (North Africa), the ancient peoples of Turkey, and Egypt (Ezekiel 38:1-6).

In I Chronicles 12:32 the Lord describes the qualities of each of the 12 tribes of Israel. Of the children of the tribe of Issachar it is written that they "were men that had understanding of the times, to know what Israel ought to do." Do we have an understanding of the times in which we are living?

Figure 51 - Modern-Day Esthers

Are we so busy with the business of surviving in this world that we are unaware that there is a divine plan and that the prophetic clock is ticking? In the bible account, the sons of Issachar *knew* the times and that *knowing* enabled them to fulfill their destiny.

Mahmoud Ahmadinejad, who was then the newly elected President of Iran, determined to squelch the revolt against the demonstrators. He made it plain that he hated the Jews, God's chosen people. He was determined to eradicate them (the little Satan) along with the United States of America (the big Satan).

Whether Ahmadinejad or his successor, Hassan Rouhani, it is immaterial to the final prophetic scene. Iran will be lined up against Israel in the end and it will be God Himself, who will deal the final death blow to the enemies of God's chosen people.

"With pestilence and with blood I will enter into judgment with him and I will rain on him and on his troops, and on the many peoples who are with him, a torrential rain, with hailstones, fire and brimstone . . . and they will know that I am the Lord" (Ezekiel 38:22-23).

We are living in exciting times! We were put here "for such a time as this." We have a destiny to fulfill and it is vital that we rise up as sons of Issachar and have an "understanding of the times."

SCRIPTURES FOR MEDITATION
(Selah – think on these things)

MONDAY: *I desire to be like the sons of Issachar who had an understanding of the times in which they lived.*

Scriptures: Proverbs 25:2; Matthew 16:1-4; 2 Timothy 2:15-19; James 1:5; Revelation 19:10.

TUESDAY: *I will be willing to stand for righteousness as did Esther.*

Scripture: Genesis 6:1-8; Esther 4:12-17; Daniel 1:8, 3:13-18; Acts 9:11-18; Revelation 2:10-11.

WEDNESDAY: *Esther stood for her people, the Jews. Today I will stand for the Jews and the land of Israel. God has said He will bless those who bless Israel.*

Scriptures: Genesis 12:1-3; Deuteronomy 7:6-8; Psalm 105:6-13, 122:6-7, 137:5-6; Jeremiah 31:35-37.

THURSDAY: *I believe I am living in the end times and therefore I am determined to make every day count for eternity!*

Scriptures: Daniel 12:2-4; Matthew 6:19-21, 24:42-47; Luke 21:24-28; I Peter 1:23-25.

FRIDAY: *I realize that walking with the Lord will require sacrifice of me. I am willing to give my all to please my Lord.*

Scriptures: Matthew 16:24-28; Luke 9:23-26; John 12:24-26; Acts 7:55-60; Hebrews 11:32-40.

SATURDAY: *I am grateful to be living in "the time of the end." I know God has put me here for such a time as this and by His grace I will fulfill my destiny.*

Scriptures: Isaiah 6:1-8, 62:6-7; Acts 17:24-28; 1 Corinthians 1:26-29; Galatians 1:11-16.

Week 38
A DIVIDED HOUSE

When football season rolls around we sometimes have a dilemma in our home and even our church. Although it's all in fun and not by any means serious, sometimes it gets a little testy; especially, when Auburn and Georgia are playing. It gets even more complicated when West Virginia gets thrown in the mix.

Charlie is a staunch Mountaineer, coming from the West Virginia hills. He truly did have a mountain-mama in "almost heaven—West Virginia."

For many years we followed West Virginia; then we moved to Georgia in the winter of '74 and along came Herschel Walker. Who in their right mind could root for the Mountaineers when they saw the 1982 Heisman Trophy winner in his No. 34 jersey jogging onto the field?

Figure 52 - A Strong Mountaineer

Enter Rob Phinazee who became our son-in-law in the 1990's. Rob is an Auburn University graduate and avid Tiger fan; I found my loyalty to the Georgia Bulldogs begin to falter, until Alan Raffield joined our family. Alan was a huge Georgia Bulldog fan and gave Charlie fits about the Mountaineers.

On the one hand, I felt I had to be loyal to Charlie's team, yet for the sake of my son-in-law and grandsons, I might have to pull for the Tigers. My own children, most of whom were raised in Georgia, are always hoping for a Bulldog win. You can see why our household gets divided at times.

But there is one thing we're all on the same page about . . . that's our belief in the Lord Jesus Christ. No division there.

This year (2017) marked the 50th Anniversary of Israel's Six Day War, in which the Jewish State of Israel reunified Jerusalem for the first time in nearly 2,000 years! Despite this monumental victory there are those who seek to divide the holy city and make the entire state of Israel return to their pre-1967 borders.

Figure 53 - Alan & Charlie

This is certainly more disturbing than whether to root for Georgia, Auburn, or the West Virginia Mountaineers. The proposed giving away of East Jerusalem to the Palestinians would set back religious freedom in Israel and no doubt cause more tension than there is at present.

Prime Minister Benjamin Netanyahu said, "The idea of a divided, split, wounded city is one we will never return to."

Psalm 83:2-5 says, "See how Your enemies are astir, how Your foes rear their heads. With cunning they conspire against Your people; they plot against those you cherish. 'Come,' they say, 'let us destroy them as a nation, that the name of Israel be remembered no more. With one mind they plot together; they form an alliance against You.'"

According to Mid-East expert, Dr. Mike Evans, "The acceptance of this vile plan would turn Israel into a living hell. The Jewish people would be forced to live next door to a state controlled by Islamic fanatics such as Hamas."

A Divided House

In January 2006 the terrorist organization, Hamas, was democratically elected to the Palestinian parliament. They have repeatedly called for terrorist attacks against Israel and have vowed to drive them into the sea. They will never recognize Israel's legal right to exist as a nation.

Figure 54 - There's no division here!

To allow Jerusalem to be divided would be the beginning of the end. History is a great teacher. Several times God had been fed up with mankind. In Noah's day the wickedness of the people brought about the destruction of all but eight people through the Flood.

Man's conniving to have a one world religion at the building of the tower of Babel caused God to confound the languages; thus, was defeated man's bid for ultimate supremacy, even against God. When Sodom and Gomorrah continued with every abominable sin imaginable, they were totally destroyed.

I believe, without a shadow of a doubt, that God is keenly interested in the affairs of men. He has called Israel the "apple of His eye." The Abrahamic Covenant is still good. "I will bless those who bless you and will curse those who curse you" (Genesis 12:3).

"Pray for the peace of Jerusalem. They shall prosper who love thee" (Psalm 122:6).

SCRIPTURES FOR MEDITATION
(Selah – think on these things)

MONDAY: *I am convinced the Word of God is true; therefore, I am convinced that God has made a covenant with Israel concerning who owns the land!*

Scriptures: Genesis 17:1-7, 12:1-3, 15:18; 1 Chronicles 16:13-19; Psalm 105:6-15; Ezekiel 37:21-28.

TUESDAY: *Despite all the dire news about our world's condition I choose to trust God and not be afraid!*

Scripture: Joshua 1:9; Psalm 23:4, 34:4-6, 94:19; Isaiah 43:1; Roman 8:38-39; 2 Timothy 1:7.

WEDNESDAY: *My loyalty is to God first, before any person or program.*

Scriptures: Deuteronomy 30:15-20; Matthew 6:33; Luke 14:25-27; John 14:15-21; 1 John 5:3.

THURSDAY: *One day, in the not too distant future, the Lord will rule from Jerusalem and the entire world will finally realize what "Peace on Earth, good will toward men" means.*

Scriptures: Isaiah 11:1-9, 35:1-10, 59:19-21, 62:1-7; Zechariah 14:1-9; Luke 2:6-19; John 16:33.

FRIDAY: *I am so thankful for the many organizations God has raised up to bless Israel. Lord, bless Jewish Voice,*

Jews for Jesus, Chosen People Ministries, Mike Evans, Christians United for Israel and so many others who are blessing Your special people.

Scriptures: 2 Chronicles 6:21, 7:14; Psalm 17:1-6; Jeremiah 29:10-14; Ephesians 1:15-23.

SATURDAY: *Although many are calling for a "One world religion" the only hope is Jesus. Jesus said that He was the only way to salvation. I will not be deceived into thinking there are many ways to God.*

Scriptures: Proverbs 26:25-26, 27:6; 2 Thessalonians 2:9-12; James 1:26; 2 Peter 2:1-3, 12-13.

Just Jerri

Week 39
WHY A BIBLE READING MARATHON?

Several months ago the Cochran community came together again to read the entire Bible from the steps of our county courthouse. People of all ages, denominations and ethnic backgrounds put aside their differences and joined in the reading of the best-selling book in the world.

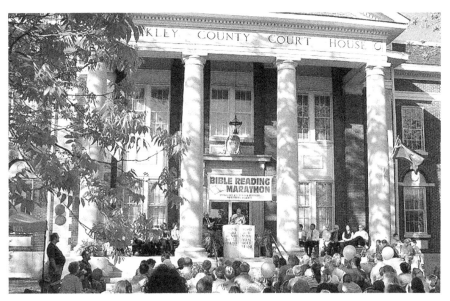

Figure 55 - The Bible Reading Marathon

Although we're living in an area referred to as the Bible belt, many Christians have never read their Bibles through from Genesis to Revelation, much less memorized any portion of Holy Writ. If we can say John 3:16 from memory we think we've really done something. The average Christian reads his bible less than 30 minutes a week.

The late Dr. Bill Bright (Campus Crusade for Christ), along with Dr. John A. Hash, Co-chaired a global movement to challenge people to read their bibles. In 1990 their goal was to enlist one billion people to read their bibles completely through. The result of this goal was the beginning of Bible

Reading Marathons from town squares, on county courthouse steps, and at state capitols.

Several years ago, the Catholic Church held a Bible Reading Marathon on TV from the Vatican in Rome. Thousands took part in this reading.

Every year since 1990 the Bible has been read in its entirety from the steps of our nation's capital in Washington, D.C. Bible Reading Marathons have been held throughout the world from India to Holland, from New Zealand to Peru, from Australia to Canada.

Figure 56 – ACLJ – Andy Ekonomou

The task of holding a marathon of this sort could never be accomplished without the support of an entire community. This year over 300 people, from 30 various churches, participated in this event.

The Bible transcends denominations, racial differences, economic and social standing. The Bible was written for all people for all time. Its message is one of the love of God and the restoration of the human race back to God through the death and resurrection of His son, Jesus Christ.

Those who have participated in our Annual Bible Marathons have shared so many stories with me of how God has touched their hearts and changed their lives by reading the Bible publicly. How thankful we should be that the laws of our land allow us the freedom of speech, provided in the first amendment, to speak forth God's Word in a public setting.

Several years ago, Mark Youngblood, a blind reader from Tabernacle Baptist Church, used a cassette recorder to do his reading. His portion began in Numbers 10. Mike Campbell his pastor cued up the cassette and the reading began: ". . . and it

Why a Bible Reading Marathon?

came to pass, when the ark set forward, that Moses said, Rise up, LORD, and let Thine enemies be scattered; and let them that hate Thee flee before Thee."

The enemy DID scatter that day in 2013. All fear left Mark. The blindness that would have been a stumbling block had been defeated and the Word of the LORD went forth in power.

Figure 57 -Mayor Pro-Tem Willie Basby

Today there are many enemies that seek to stop us from doing God's work. Worse than any physical blindness, spiritual blindness threatens the masses today. They are blind to the God who loves them and sent His only begotten Son to die for them; they rant and rave against the Bible.

During this past year we have heard story after story from the Middle East where Christians have lost their lives because of their faith in Christ. Some have been beheaded, while others have been crucified. ISIS marches on, planting their flag of hate and murder, declaring that the place where their flag is planted belongs to them.

Last year (2016) we faced a challenge about holding the Bible Reading Marathon at the courthouse. Thankfully Jay Sekulow, from the American Center for Law and Justice, took our case and sent letters to our Bleckley County Commissioner and our Bleckley County Attorney unequivocally showing that we had the legal right to read Scriptures from our courthouse.

The naysayers cry, "separation of church and state" when that phrase is not even in our U.S. Constitution. They want to get every reference to God out of our school systems, our government, and our lives. I'm wondering why they don't move to China or Russia if they want to live in a godless society.

During the week of the Bible Reading Marathon the crowds constantly change in number. Sometimes many are listening and at other times only a few, especially in the early morning hours. However, we know there is always One listening who never misses a word. His Name is the Lord God Almighty. He's always there and always pleased that His people are making time to do something that really blesses Him.

So why do we hold a public Bible Reading Marathon? The answer is very simple. GOD LIKES IT!! That's good enough for me. "Thou hast magnified Thy Word above all Thy Name" (Ps. 138:2).

SCRIPTURES FOR MEDITATION

(Selah – think on these things)

MONDAY: *I'm so thankful our country's laws protect the public reading of the Scriptures. I am determined to do what I can to continue this annual event and encourage other communities to do likewise.*

Scriptures: Matthew 4:4; John 6:63, 8:31-32, 14:23-25; Acts 20:32; Romans 15:4; 2 Timothy 3:15-17.

TUESDAY: *I cannot successfully live as a Christian without a steady diet of the Word of God. I will do my best to make reading the Bible a priority in my life.*

Scripture: Genesis 39:2-6; 1 Kings 2:1-4; Psalm 1:1-3; Proverbs 16:3; Philippians 4:13.

WEDNESDAY: *Since God speaks to us through His Word it would be foolish of me not to read it every day.*

Scriptures: Deuteronomy 8:1-6; Matthew 13:18-23; John 16:13-14; James 1:22-25.

THURSDAY: *The Word of God is nourishment to my soul and so I will eat it every day.*

Scriptures: Jeremiah 15:16; John 6:63; 1Timothy 4:6; 1 Peter 2:2; Revelation 10:10.

FRIDAY: *I desire to be a person of faith and therefore I must fill my mind with the Word of God.*

Scriptures: Proverbs 28:26; Romans 10:17, 12:1-2; Ephesians 4:22-32; Philippians 4:8.

SATURDAY: *I can't go wrong if I make the Word of God my life's compass.*

Scriptures: Job 23:12; Psalm 119:105; 2 Corinthians 3:18; 2 Timothy 3:16-17; 1 Peter 1:3-5.

Week 40
MORE THAN A CASE OF SPILLED MILK

The clerks at the registers were dumbfounded when a customer told them she couldn't find any gallon jugs of milk in the dairy department with lids on them. Surely the elderly lady was only joking.

But joking, she was not! When they went to check on the situation; they were surprised to discover thirty-seven jugs of milk had been opened and the lids were scattered on the shelves.

Upon further investigation, the managers reviewed the store security video tapes, and saw a little boy working just as fast as he could, taking lids off the milk jugs.

Unable to sell the damaged merchandise, store personnel had to pour out the milk. At $3.59 a pop that was a lot of spilled milk! Needless to say, one little boy either has a guilty conscience, a sore bottom, or both.

Figure 58 – BRM Volunteer-Buddy G.W. Roberson

I was reminded of the Scripture that says, "The eyes of the LORD are in every place, beholding the evil and the good" (Prov. 5:21). That verse along with, "Be sure your sin will find you out" (Num. 32:23), would also be appropriate in this instance.

On the flip-side of the watchful eye scenario is the fact that God is also watching when we do good deeds, whether we're being taped or not. During one of our Annual Bible Reading Marathons, a participant was somewhat disappointed when it came to his turn to read the bible and looking out over the courthouse plaza he realized he was all alone.

A worker sitting at the registration table realized what was happening and she tried to encourage him with the truth that God was listening and watching. In fact, God is mindful of everything we do and we don't need the attention or praise of man to keep us faithful to Him.

Figure 59 – BRM Volunteer-Jim Parks

Jesus told us not to let our right hand know what our left hand is doing. The principle of doing all for the glory of God, whether or not we are ever recognized by man, is a basic principle for Christian living. If we need a pat on the back for our service to God, we're doing it for the wrong motive.

A few years ago, as we tallied the registration slips from the Bible Reading Marathon, we were thrilled to see that thirty-one churches participated, either by helping with the menial behind the scenes tasks or by actually publicly reading the Bible.

One of the strongest backers of the Bible Reading Marathon was retired MGC educator Jim Parks. Jim's tireless effort in encouraging readers from his church (Southside Baptist), working for hours and hours at the registration table, and offering to help wherever needed has not gone unnoticed by the Lord. In fact, our dear friend went to be with the Lord this past June 2017, and I imagine he heard a loud, "Well done, thou good and faithful servant. Enter thou into the joy of thy Lord!" (Matthew 25:23)

On the Wednesday night before the BRM begins, our church (New Life Church of God) comes together and puts up tents and tables and makes sure we have plenty of bottled water to pass out to thirsty readers.

Buddy Roberson (a Bleckley County employee) from Immanuel Missionary Baptist Church does his best (on his own time) to see that the pulpit, chairs and audio equipment are set up. Buddy would never brag about anything he does, but like so many who help, he is seen by God and that, in itself, is more meaningful to Buddy than the praise of men.

In 2017, we were honored to have as our guest speaker on opening night, Don Giles, President of our Bleckley Christian Learning Center (BCLC). Don is an outstanding Christian and has been very instrumental in getting bible classes started in our public-school system. We enjoyed hearing him share about the value of bible reading in his own life.

Figure 60 – BCLC Pres. Don Giles

I've heard that when you start to mention names you can really get into trouble, because surely someone will be omitted. I confess that scores have been omitted because of *JUST JERRI* column space, but I'm sure folks would rather hear words of commendation from the Lord Himself!

And a very special thanks to our wonderful Lord, Who makes this whole week of blessing possible. I'm so glad He says that His Word will not return to Him void. It will accomplish that which He pleases and will prosper in the place where He sends it. (Isaiah 55:11)

SCRIPTURES FOR MEDITATION

(Selah – think on these things)

MONDAY: *I am thankful God has His eye on me!*

Scriptures: 1 Samuel 16:7; Job 34:21; Psalm 32:8, 34:21; Proverbs 15:3; 2 Corinthians 8:21; 1 Peter 3:12.

TUESDAY: *Knowing God sees everything makes me realize that His judgment will be righteous.*

Scripture: Ezekiel 5:15; John 5:24; Acts 12:23; Romans 1:18-24, 11:7-8; 1 Corinthians 11:30-32.

WEDNESDAY: *If I live my life for God's glory and not my own I can be assured that He will be pleased.*

Scriptures: Psalm 96:1-9, 115:1; John 14:13; 2 Thessalonians 1:12; 1 Peter 4:11; Revelation 15:4.

THURSDAY: *I may fail in recognizing those who have done things for me or others, but I am confident that they will be recognized by God Himself.*

Scriptures: Ruth 2:11-12; Isaiah 40:10, 52:12; Matthew 10:40-42; Mark 9:41; Hebrews 6:10.

FRIDAY: *I am so grateful for the many friends I have in my life. Lord, help me today to be a good friend to others.*

Scriptures: Proverbs 16:7, 27:17; Ecclesiastes 4:9-12; John 15:12-15; 1 Thessalonians 5:11-13; Hebrews 10:24.

SATURDAY: *I am so grateful we are able to teach bible classes in our public schools because the Word of God is incorruptible. I know it will take root in the hearts of these children.*

Scriptures: Deuteronomy 4:9-10, 6:5-9, 11:19; Proverbs 22:6; Matthew 19:13-15; Ephesians 6:4.

Week 41
I'M STANDING ON THE INSIDE

The all too familiar scene took place in an attorney's office. The deceased was speaking by way of a pre-recorded video as the expectant heirs sit nervously in their seats.

"And I leave my entire fortune to my grandson, Billy." As the startling news was revealed, Billy sat up with amazement on his face. "However," the grandmother continued, "he can only receive the inheritance if he learns to dress himself better."

The next scene in the TV commercial is of Billy making tracks to the Burlington Coat Factory. After trying on dozens of new outfits he makes his way back to the attorney's office, only to discover that Grandma is alive and well!

With all the relatives grinning as they stand beside Grandma she says, "We had to do something to make you dress better Billy! And you look so good you probably don't even need my money."

Oh, if only a change of clothes could really make a difference in the inner makeup of a person. I'm reminded of the story of the man who cleaned up his hog and got her ready for the county fair. The hog walked proudly beside the farmer with her skin gleaming pink and a ribbon around her neck. With a dash of perfume applied behind her pink ears, she even smelled good.

Alas, at the first mud hole they approached on the way to the fair, the sow bolted and jumped in with all fours. Rolling in the mud, the true nature of the pig was never more obvious.

Folks today are convinced through the media and through erroneous teachings that if they dress the part they can be something that they're really not. If you believe the ads; you'll know that if you drink Coke, things will really go better for you. If you drink Pepsi, you're a young and progressive thinker. If you drink a Bud, you'll be popular and surrounded with friends.

Schools of humanistic philosophy are always trying to get you to have a better self-image. We hear this taught in our schools and promoted by psychiatrists and psychologists. Just think you're great and you'll be great. See yourself as successful and you'll be successful. Sad to say, some of the most successful people in our world today are the most miserable. Somewhere along the line success got confused with happiness.

In many churches the outward appearance is stressed rather than an inward change of nature. They say you have to have the right look about you to be spiritual. Some on the extreme end insist that holiness is synonymous with no make-up, jewelry, or bobbed hair. Others more lenient in these areas still insist that, if your skirt isn't a certain length or you have a tattoo on your body that you can't be spiritual.

Figure 61 – All Cleaned Up

The outward appearance is not always indicative of what is going on inside a person. Johnny was such a bad little boy. His mother kept telling him to sit down in church and would pull him back onto the pew each time he stood up. Finally, in exasperation he said, "I may be sitting down on the outside, but I'm standing up on the inside!"

When I was in the real estate business I was always cautious not to judge a person's ability to purchase property by the way they looked when they came into my office.

Some of the wealthiest people I've ever sold a house to would never make it on the town's "best dressed list," but if they took out their bank books to compare with others you would be surprised at the bottom figure!

I'm Standing on the Inside

I'm so glad God doesn't grant our inheritance on the basis of how we look on the outside. The day will come when there will be the final reading of the will. On that day the true intent and motives of the heart will be judged. The true sons and daughters of God will be granted an inheritance far beyond their wildest imagination.

Figure 62 – Right Back Into The Mud

"Eye has not seen, nor ear heard, neither has it entered into the heart of man what God has prepared for those who love him" (1 Cor. 2:9).

SCRIPTURES FOR MEDITATION

(Selah – think on these things)

MONDAY: *Lord, help me not to judge people by outward appearances.*

Scriptures: Isaiah 29:13; Matthew 7:16-20, 12:33-37; Luke 6:43-45; 2 Corinthians 11:13-15.

TUESDAY: *I'm so grateful that the Lord loved me and saved me, even in my sinful condition. I will serve Him all my days.*

Scripture: Jeremiah 31:3; Acts 10:34-35; Roman 5:8, 11:29-36; 2 Corinthians 2:9; Ephesians 1:3-12; 1 John 4:10.

WEDNESDAY: *For those who turn back from following the Lord there is only misery. Lord, please help me to walk close to You.*

Scriptures: Genesis 19:22-26; Psalm 41:9; Proverbs 26:11; John 19:10-11; 2 Peter 2:21-22; Jude 1:10-11.

THURSDAY: *Not all who say they are Christians are true believers. Lord, please help me to have discernment.*

Scriptures: Hosea 14:9; Malachi 3:16-18; Matthew 7:21-23; Philippians 1:9-10; 1 John 4:1-6.

FRIDAY: *The best image I can have of myself is to agree with what God says about me in His Word.*

Scriptures: Deuteronomy 28:1-14; Acts 1:8; Romans 8:37, 12:3; 2 Corinthians 5:17-21; 1 John 4:4.

SATURDAY: *The things of this world are passing. Only what is of God will last forever. Lord, please help me to lift my eyes to major on things that are eternal.*

Scriptures: Psalm 121:1-2; Matthew 6:19-21; 2 Corinthians 4:16-18; 2 Peter 3:8-13; Revelation 21:1-5.

Week 42

BURIED IN TIME

BOOM!!

The house reverberated with an unusually loud, supersonic noise. The children and I ran to Charlie, asking, "What was that?"

He was just as much in the dark as the rest of us.

The year was 1973 and we were living in California. Dressed in our jeans and overalls, we were getting ready to work in our small, backyard garden. As we rushed outside, to see if perhaps a car had hit our house, we saw our neighbors pouring out of their houses looking just as puzzled as we were. As we looked, we could plainly see that the house directly across the street had all the windows blown out, by what appeared to be a bomb blast.

Figure 63 - The Bomb at the Railroad Yard

That's exactly what it was!

Less than a mile from our subdivision and across Interstate 80, the Southern Pacific Railroad had suffered a major accident. A railroad car, loaded with live ammunition, had caught fire and some of the contents had exploded! Houses close to the site were leveled, buildings were burning and people were milling about in stunned disbelief. The local civil defense unit quickly set up headquarters in a nearby park and began the process of evacuating everyone from their houses and businesses for miles around.

In an intersection near our house, a live bomb had landed. Believe me, they didn't have to tell us twice to evacuate. In all there were approximately 7,000 missing bombs that had to be located.

Figure 64 - Charlie & Jerri at former home in CA

When all the dust settled, it turned out that although there were injuries and the dollar loss was in the millions, no one was killed. Due to the fact our house was closer to the interstate embankment; the concussion waves passed over our house and hit the houses across from us. The outer walls of our stucco house were seriously cracked and the permanent section of our sliding glass door had moved and then returned to its original position, trapping a portion of our draperies between the window frame and the wall.

Eventually all those who suffered damages were compensated by Southern Pacific Railroad. We repaired our houses and went on with our lives.

In 1997 I received an E-mail from a girlfriend in California. Her letter in part read, "They were excavating around the train yard and they found an unexploded bomb from the 1973 train accident. The bomb had been buried for 24 years. Around 9:30 last night the feds detonated it!"

Buried in time!

You know friend, sin is like that. Bitterness, anger, resentment; you can bury it, but unless it's defused through the blood of Jesus Christ, someday it will go off and great will be the disaster.

Things may look peaceful on the surface of your life, but do you have a bomb buried beneath the façade? Are there people you can't stand? Are there people who have hurt you and instead of forgiving them, you have buried those angry feelings? You know it's there and you think if you just don't say anything no one will ever know. No one will ever be hurt.

One day it will surface and then what? Pressures come. A weak moment... and BOOM!! You explode! In Numbers 32:23 it says, "Be sure your sin will find you out."

How much better it will be for you, and everyone around you, if you turn that time bomb over to Jesus. Let Him give you the victory over your buried sins. Today, if you will open your heart to Him and say, "Lord, do I have anything buried in my life that needs to be taken out and cleansed?" Trust me, He'll show you. How liberating it is to know the forgiveness that He can bring. I pray you'll take the time to do it now... before the bomb explodes!

As a footnote on this Just Jerri article I wanted you to know that when I was asked to write a weekly column and told the Cochran Journal editor, Judy Sherling, that I would do it, I seriously wondered what I would write about. When I got home, on that very day I said I would write a column each week, I had the message from Karen Lyman about the unexploded bomb! I knew immediately what I would write about. This was my first column in 1997. God wasn't fooling around when he told me to do this. I definitely got the message . . . loud and clear!

SCRIPTURES FOR MEDITATION
(Selah – think on these things)

MONDAY: *I know that nothing is hidden from God. I will therefore keep short accounts by confessing my sins and resolving to live a holy life before Him.*

Scriptures: Genesis 16:13; Job 31:1-6, 34:21-23; Psalm 66:5-7, 139:1-6; Proverbs 15:3; Daniel 2:20-22.

TUESDAY: *I know that unforgiveness is a person's own poison. Therefore, I will walk in forgiveness.*

Scripture: Matthew 6:1-15; 18:23-35; Luke 23:34; Ephesians 4:31-32; Colossians 3:12-14.

WEDNESDAY: *Although I may be aware that people may not like me, I will continue to love and pray for them.*

Scriptures: Proverbs 16:7; Matthew 5:44; Romans 12:18-21; Colossians 1:21; 1 John 4:7-11.

THURSDAY: *I am so thankful that God accepts me and loves me as His very own child.*

Scriptures: Hosea 2:19-20; John 6:37; Romans 15:7; Ephesians 1:7; 1 Timothy 1:12-15.

FRIDAY: *I will come to God as honestly as I can and ask Him to show me anything hidden in my heart that is not of Him.*

Scriptures: Psalm 139:23-24; Matthew 5:8; Ephesians 4:22-25; Colossians 3:8-10; 2 Timothy 2:15.

SATURDAY: *I'm so grateful for God's protection over me and my loved ones. I will continue to plead the BLOOD OF JESUS over our household and those of our children, grandchildren, and great-grandchildren.*

Scriptures: Exodus 12:13; Proverbs 31:21; Colossians 1:20; Hebrews 9:22; 1 Peter 1:18-19; Revelation 12:11.

Week 43
WHERE THE TREE FALLS

In 2006 Alan our sixteen-year-old, brought a whole new meaning to the verse in Ecclesiastes that states, "Where the tree falleth, there shall it lay" (Eccl. 11:3).

Trying to keep the boy busy during the hot summer months, I decided to have him clear some brush near the back of our house. First, there was the need for a bow saw, clippers and gloves, so off to the hardware store I go. That all taken care of and seeing that he and his buddy were clipping away, I went to the grocery store.

Now you have to realize that my trips to the store are not quickies. Down one of the aisles was an old friend I hadn't seen in ages. During the course of our twenty minutes or so conversation we covered everything from her daughter's marriage this past Easter, to the exciting time my pastor and I had recently when we led a man to Christ in my office.

Figure 65 – Downed Trees Everywhere

Of course, I had to stop and get ice for the Gatorade I had purchased. There's nothing like cold Gatorade to keep two teenagers working. It was at the convenience store that I happened to meet up with a local pastor who drives a delivery truck on the side.

Another twenty minutes ticked by while we rejoiced together over the 2006 Bible Reading Marathon and how God was working in our community. These were all positive but lengthy conversations that took place on my grocery trip.

Oh, did I mention that Charlie had prayed for the boys' safety before I left the house and while he was at it, threw in a request that God would give us grace and PATIENCE?

When I returned home, it is hard to describe the scene of devastation that lay before my eyes. No, it wasn't a tornado. Could it have been a hurricane? Maybe it was a dream, or more likely a nightmare!

Dashing into the house, I asked Charlie if he had seen what the kids had done. He replied by saying he had just gotten home from taking the chainsaw to the neighboring town of Eastman for repairs and no, he had no idea what they had done.

The boys were so proud of their work. They had cut down just about every tree in the area where I had instructed them to cut only the brush. The oak trees were 15-20 years old. Alan proudly exclaimed that he had left the pines, one of which is dead! I think it's going to take me awhile to get over this one.

Figure 66 – A Brand New Look

I never imagined when I taught Ecclesiastes in a Sunday school class at the Jeffersonville Church of God, that the Scripture that had become one of my favorites, would come back to test me so severely.

When Solomon penned those words, it was a metaphorical way of stating the fact that there is no sense in crying over spilled milk. "Where the tree falls, there shall it lay." Most likely in modern day lingo he would have said, "Get over it, honey. What's done is done."

I managed to keep my cool, made a big lunch for the kids and even smiled when Alan asked if he could knock off at four o'clock and go to his friend's house. I reminded myself about the positive side of this whole debacle—the chainsaw had been taken to the repair shop. Can you even imagine what could have happened, if those two teenagers had had a working chainsaw? I shudder to think.

Okay. So, I can't put the trees back on the stumps. Neither can I change anything else in my life, whether good or bad. Paul puts it this way in Philippians: "Forgetting those things which are behind, and reaching forth unto those things which are before, I press toward the mark for the prize of the high calling of God in Christ Jesus" (Phil. 3:13-14).

Today, instead of a barren area of downed trees there is a beautiful herb garden. God can make a new picture for us, even when things happen that we can't fix. We couldn't put a single tree back on its stump, but with some elbow grease and time we could have a whole new look . . . even a better look than before.

Do you have some downed trees in your life, situations that you would give anything if they had gone in a different direction, choices you wish you hadn't made and can't undo? Quit looking at the past. Ask the Lord to help you to look forward to Him. He will give you the grace to make it past every stump, and He may even give you a smile and a new landscape on your way.

SCRIPTURES FOR MEDITATION

(Selah – think on these things)

MONDAY: *I am grateful for God's grace toward me when I do foolish things. Lord, please help me to have grace for others.*

Scriptures: John 1:17; Romans 1:1-6, 3:23-24; 2 Corinthians 12:8-9; Ephesians 2:8-9; 4:7; 1 Peter 4:10.

TUESDAY: *I will not allow myself to wallow in self-pity over the mistakes I've made in the past. By God's grace I will rejoice today and leave the future to Him.*

Scripture: Psalm 34:22, 103:10-11; Isaiah 43:25; John 3:17, 8:1-11; Romans 8:1; 1 John 3:20-22.

WEDNESDAY: *When things happen that I have no control over, I will trust the Lord to turn circumstances to His good and His glory.*

Scriptures: Zephaniah 3:9-20; 2 Corinthians 4:16-17; Philippians 4:6-7; James 1:2-5; 1 Peter 1:5-7.

THURSDAY: *I am so thankful God can take our messes and turn them into a message for Him.*

Scriptures: Job 42:12-17; Isaiah 40:1-2; Romans 5:3-5, 12:12; 1 Thessalonians 5:18; 1 Peter 2:9.

FRIDAY: *I will remember that choices can oftentimes bring seriously bad consequences. Lord, help me to choose the good and right way.*

Scriptures: Joshua 24:15; Proverbs 1:28-33; Mark 10:17-27; Luke 12:16-21; Galatians 6:6-9.

SATURDAY: *I will remember that life is full of changes, but God never changes. He will always be there when I need Him and He will always love me.*

Scriptures: 1 Samuel 15:29; Psalm 18:30, 33:11; Malachi 3:6; Hebrews 13:8; James 1:17.

Week 44
HAPPY BIRTHDAY, BERTHA!

Bertha Jenkins, full of life and optimism, is an officer at the Bleckley Probation Detention Center in Cochran. This past week she shared an amazing story of personal victory with me and I want to pass it on to you, my readers.

Bertha celebrated, and I do mean celebrated her 57th birthday this past September. Ordinarily, a 57th birthday is no big deal to most folks, but for Bertha, number 57 was big!

People might think Bertha's family had been under some kind of curse when they hear her story. You see, Bertha's grandmother, mother, sister, and aunt all died at age 56. This sounds uncanny, to be sure, but nonetheless it happened. As a result of their identical ages at death, the closer it came to her birthday this year, the harder Bertha had to fight the despair and anxiety that tried to overwhelm her.

Figure 67 - Happy Birthday Bertha!

She shared with me how she refused to accept death as inevitable. Every time the devil would whisper his negative words in her ear she would rebuke him and tell him she was not under the curse of death. She reminded him she was a free woman under the protection of the blood of Jesus Christ!

The night before her birthday she had worked at the center. When her shift ended, she got in her car and began the drive home. Satan immediately jumped in the car with her. This time he started his whisper campaign in earnest. "Bertha, you won't be driving this way again after tonight. You're going to die. It will all be over."

She thought of her grandmother, her mother and her sister, who had all died of colon cancer at 56. She thought of her aunt who had a fatal heart attack at age 56. And then she thought of Jesus. "Devil," she shouted. "You're a liar. Now, get out of my car!"

Figure 68 – Victory Through the Blood

Bertha went to bed that night with a prayer on her lips. Trusting in Jesus, she fell fast asleep. Morning came and with it, the realization that she was 57. She hurriedly went into her prayer closet where she and Jesus had been having some awesome times together. "Lord," she prayed, "excuse me a minute. I have to do something." Addressing Satan, she said, "I told you Devil, you're a liar. I'm still here, now you go on and get out!"

No wonder Bertha beams with the joy of the Lord radiating from her face. She says every day is a beautiful gift from God. She knows, first hand, the power of prayer and the efficacy of the blood of Jesus Christ.

I like Bertha's positive attitude. This is a great example for all of us. We all need to latch on to the promises in God's Word like Bertha has done.

In Galatians 3:13 we are told that Christ has redeemed us from the curse of the law, having become a curse for us. John, the beloved apostle, tells us that we overcome Satan through the blood of the lamb (Jesus), by the word of our testimony, and by not loving our lives, even unto death (Rev. 12:11). How about you? Are you living in victory like Bertha?

SCRIPTURES FOR MEDITATION

(Selah – think on these things)

MONDAY: *I am so thankful that God has redeemed me from the curse of the law.*

Scriptures: Habakkuk 2:4; Romans 9:31-34; Galatians 1:7-8, 3:10-14; Hebrews 8:7-13.

TUESDAY: *I am so thankful for the blood of Christ. The old song, "There is Power in the Blood" is a reality in my life.*

Scripture: Ephesians 1:6-7; Hebrews 9:11-15; 1 John 1:7, 5:6; Revelation 5:9-10.

WEDNESDAY: *I do not have to fear death because God is in control of my destiny.*

Scriptures: John 14:1-6; 2 Corinthians 5:6-8; Philippians 1:21-23; Hebrews 2:14-15.

THURSDAY: *I am so thankful that the Word of God carries the power to defeat the Devil at every turn.*

Scriptures: Romans 8:38-39, 16:20; Colossians 2:13-15; 1 John 3:8; Revelation 12:11.

FRIDAY: *Today, I will share with others the Good News that they can live in victory because of the blood of Jesus.*

Scriptures: Deuteronomy 20:4; 1 Corinthians 10:13, 15:57-58; Ephesians 6:13.

SATURDAY: *I refuse all forms of spiritual and physical laziness. I will be about the Master's business today!*

Scriptures: Proverbs 6:9-11, 10:4-5; Luke 2:49; Ephesians 5:14-16; 2 Thessalonians 3:10-13.

Week 45
THE ROCKS WILL CRY OUT!

Messages from God are found in the strangest places. Recently, while shopping, a friend and I were talking about a challenging sermon from a pie plate! My friend had bought a pie and when she went to wash the pie plate she discovered a message printed on the pie tin. It said: "Everyone you meet will live forever. The question is where?"

In checking out the pie company I learned that the pie tins bearing these messages are dubbed "personality pans." Who would have thought of putting a message for God on a pie tin? Truly the Lord is determined to get His Word out.

Figure 69 – Pro-Lifers at Mt. Rushmore

Have you ever noticed the spiritual messages on tee-shirts, bumper stickers, yellow page advertisements and even on neon signs? We're living in an age when virtually no one will have an excuse for not knowing about God. Even if you couldn't read a word, all you have to do is look up and see that "the heavens declare the glory of God and the firmament shows His handiwork.

In 2006 pro-family supporters met at the Mt. Rushmore National Monument for a rally in support of an amendment that would stop all abortions. They called the rally: "The Rocks Cry Out."

As they met beneath the imposing granite carvings of Washington, Jefferson, T. Roosevelt, and Lincoln they tried to inspire the crowd and the nation to return to the traditional values of morality and life. Despite their efforts the amendment was defeated by ten percent of South Dakota voters.

Figure 70 – Rocks by Martha Lee Francis

Jesus talked about the silent witnesses of creation. He said if we don't praise Him the rocks will cry out (Luke 19:28-40). His challenge to us as believers is to give voice to our belief;

but if we don't, He will make sure the message is relayed to mankind even if He has to use a rock or a pie tin!

The last verse in the book of Psalms says: "Let everything that hath breath praise the Lord. Praise ye the Lord." That doesn't seem to be just a suggestion, but a very strong instruction to the people of God to give Him the praise that is due Him. Think about it . . . we could not take a single breath were it not for our gracious God allowing us to live another day.

And what are we living for? Is it just for pleasure or for gaining more stuff? Are we just taking up space waiting for life to carry us a little farther? Are we fulfilling the purpose that God has designed for us?

While visiting in Southern California I was blessed to visit a church where the pastor spoke about the need to pursue our God ordained purpose in life.

In his message he said, "Everything you have accumulated you will one day leave behind, but everything you've given for the kingdom of God will be waiting for you in Heaven when you get there. We are investing in eternity when we give our lives for the kingdom of God."

Shirley Reeves, my friend who found the message on the pie tin, told me that she couldn't get the message out of her mind. "Jerri, just think . . . everyone we meet will live forever." It is a sobering message. The pie tin has spoken and the question hangs in the air . . . The question is . . . where will they live?

Our purpose as Christians is to give out the message about Christ. If we don't do our job then the rocks . . . and the pie tins . . . will cry out!

SCRIPTURES FOR MEDITATION
(Selah – think on these things)

MONDAY: *Eternity is forever and ever therefore I must do what I can for God while I can.*

Scriptures: 1 Chronicles 16:34-36; Psalm 90:2-6, 102:25-27; Isaiah 51:6-8; Peter 3:8.

TUESDAY: *I don't need a rock to praise God for me. I determine to give God the praise He is worthy of.*

Scripture: Exodus 15:2; Deuteronomy 10:21; Psalm 75:1; Jeremiah 20:13; Daniel 2:20-23.

WEDNESDAY: *Lord, please help me to be a good advertisement for Your kingdom.*

Scriptures: Matthew 5:14-16; Luke 2:17-18; John 3:30; Acts 1:8, 4:20; Romans 1:16; 1 Peter 3:15.

THURSDAY: *God is declaring His greatness through all creation.*

Scriptures: Job 12:7-10; Psalm 19:1-6, 96:11-12, 148:1-13; Isaiah 43:18-20; Romans 1:20.

FRIDAY: *The only lasting treasures we can keep are those which are laid up in Heaven. Help me Lord, to lay up the true treasures that will endure forever.*

Scriptures: Matthew 6:19-24, 19:21-22; Luke 12:15, 33-34, 14:33; 1 Timothy 6:17-19.

SATURDAY: *Lord, please help me today to fulfill my purpose here on Earth.*

Scriptures: Job 22:21-301; Psalm 138:8; Matthew 5:13-16; Romans 12:2; Ephesians 1:11-12; 2Timothy 1:9.

Week 46
LEGAL OR MORAL?

We used to have some pretty lively discussions around the dinner table when Charlie's mom stayed with us. My mother-in-law, who was in her eighties at the time, took the lead one night. "Jerri, there have always been abortions; you just can't legislate morality." Naturally I agreed. I wasn't going to get on the wrong side of *my* mother-in-law!

After mom went to bed that night I did some research on the Internet and sure enough she was right! Women have been having abortions for centuries. In fact, in the first century there was intense heated debate over this issue. The question, "When does life begin?" was hotly argued.

Figure 71 - Jerri's Mom, Pauline

Since Mom was a "dyed in the wool" Clinton fan, I decided to back off and not press my pro-life views with her. Mom really loved the Lord and to her, abortion was strictly a political issue. I wasn't so sure . . ..

Case in point: A young teenage girl, for now, I'll just call her Grace, got pregnant. She lived in a small town where teenage pregnancy, especially if you were unwed like Grace, was simply a disgrace.

Since you rarely heard about illegitimate births where Grace lived, no doubt a lot of back room abortions were being performed. It was important to Grace's parents and to other leaders of the community, to live an "upright life." A young teenager like Grace would be looked down on for getting pregnant. A respected place in the community would be out of the question for her. Even worse, her parents would be shunned by the church folks for having a daughter like her!

Grace's boyfriend was going to stick by her. Abortion didn't even come up in their conversation. Of course, at first, he considered not continuing their relationship because of the pregnancy, but he truly loved her. He wrestled with the situation and made up his mind. No matter what anybody thought, they would have this baby.

When Grace and her boyfriend went anywhere together you could see heads turn. Her best friend didn't want to be seen with her. The women in the church sewing circle began to shun Grace's mother. Grace's father noticed the change in the men in town. Once respected, he was now ignored. Abortion would have been an easy out for Grace . . . especially in her early trimester.

Figure 72 - Jerri (middle) L-Doug - R-Dwight Bros.

But Grace held her head high. The baby (she never referred to it as a "fetus") was growing and she could feel his little feet pushing and kicking. Her boyfriend could feel him too. When he laid his hand on her stomach, the wonder of the life within her absolutely amazed him. Who cared what everyone thought? They were already in love with this little person within her.

Figure 73 - The Gift of God

One evening the labor pains started. Her swollen face was now contorted with the agony of her contractions. She hadn't expected it to hurt so much. The baby was coming. She held the hand of her beloved and squeezed . . . hard. It would soon be over he assured her. Wiping her brow, he whispered words of love and encouragement.

Then, as if in a moment, the pain was gone. The baby cried lustily. Oh, if those who had wagged their tongues could have seen the joy in this scene. Even those who favored partial birth abortion, up to the last stages of pregnancy, would have been ashamed of themselves. This baby, as all babies, was meant to live!

Tenderly laying the baby in Grace's arms, he then kissed her lightly on the cheek, "We'll name him Jesus, just as the angel said."

With a smile on her face, and looking deeply into Joseph's eyes, Mary said, "Yes, His name shall be Jesus."

SCRIPTURES FOR MEDITATION
(Selah – think on these things)

MONDAY: *I am so glad that God values life. I will promote His values over the world's values any time!*

Scriptures: Genesis 9:5-6; Psalm 8:4-5; Proverbs 6:16-19; Matthew 6:26; Galatians 1:15.

TUESDAY: *I'm so grateful my mother chose life over abortion. I live by the grace of God and I will seek to lead the way for others.*

Scripture: Genesis 9:1-7; Job 31:15; Psalms 22:9-10, 139:13-16; John 10:10; Colossians 3:12.

WEDNESDAY: *I appreciate those who help women choose life over death for their unborn children. I will pray for them and encourage them in the fight for life.*

Scriptures: Deuteronomy 27:25; Proverbs 24:11-12; Jeremiah 1:4-5; 1 Corinthians 3:16-17.

THURSDAY: *Children are a blessing from the Lord. Dear Father, help me to appreciate the blessings You have given me. Please lead and guide them throughout their lives and receive them one day into glory!*

Scriptures: Psalm 127:3-5; Proverbs 22:6; Isaiah 54:13; Matthew 18:10; Mark 9:36-37.

FRIDAY: *Dear Lord, help me keep a sweet and non-judgmental spirit when those I talk with have opinions different from mine.*

Scriptures: Matthew 7:1-5; Luke 6:31-42; Romans 2:1-3, 14:1-13; Galatians 6:1-6; James 4:11-12.

Legal or Moral?

SATURDAY: *I'm so thankful that God sent His only begotten Son into our world in such a humble manner. I pray my life will reflect His life in all I do today.*

Scriptures: Proverbs 11:2, 29:23; Romans 12:16; Ephesians 4:2; Philippians 2:3; Colossians 3:12.

Week 47
NOTHING NEW UNDER THE SUN

A few years ago, I was intrigued by an AOL news article describing a recent White House conference call. Instead of reporters hearing Secretary of State Hillary Clinton and National Security Adviser Jim Jones informing them about foreign policy and the newest security threats, they were greeted by suggestive comments on a phone sex line.

A woman's voice invited the callers to satisfy any hidden desires by using the sex phone line services. She told them they had come to the right place if they felt "like getting nasty."

Apparently, the White House aide had mistyped the 800-dial in number. Under Bush's administration in 2007 a similar mistake was made. Instead of an aide misdialing, it was Bush himself. The former President had accidentally contacted a Texas-based group that provides Christian education.

Sex phone lines are only the tip of the pornography iceberg. Years ago, sexual predators and perverts got their kicks by sneaking into peep shows in the seamier parts of towns and cities. Today the Internet is swamped with websites offering every type of

Figure 74 – Horrific Texts On Cell Phones Today

perversion imaginable. One of today's growing concerns is *sexting*.

According to the website, "The Thoughtful Christian *Sexting* is the popular name for the act of sending, receiving, or forwarding sexually suggestive photos via a text message on a cell phone or posting pictures on social networking sites such as Facebook or Myspace."

Research has shown that technology will increase the likelihood that a teenager will share sexually suggestive material or nude photos, and that many of the teens who post this material have other problems with decision making, lack supportive role-models, or exhibit similar behaviors in real life.

To read the comments teenagers make about this latest fad will make you sick. Many of our teenagers today are in serious trouble, but let's face it; they haven't had many Godly role models to follow.

Ezekiel described a similar situation several thousand years ago. In a vision God brought him to the temple in Jerusalem. He looked and saw a hole in the temple wall and was told to dig. Soon he discovered a doorway. He was appalled at what he saw when he went inside.

Figure 75 – There Is Forgiveness with God

Portrayed all over the walls were detestable drawings. In front of the walls were the religious elite of Israel. Each was holding censers with fragrant clouds of incense rising. They were saying, "The Lord does not see us." It was no wonder that the entire nation was going down the tubes into perversion and idolatry. Their leaders were paving the way (Ezekiel 8).

Today the pornographic drawings are not on physical walls, but on the walls of young, impressionable minds. Our teens didn't start these abominable practices. Sadly, we adults must assume the responsibility. We were given a charge to protect our children. Instead we have allowed the courts, under the guise of free speech, to allow anything and everything.

Ezekiel foresaw judgment coming because of the ungodliness of his nation. As his vision progressed in chapter 9 he saw an angel who was told to go throughout the city and put a mark on the foreheads of those who grieved and lamented over the situation. Those who had the mark of God were to be spared. Friend, when God judges our nation, will you be found with His mark in your heart? "Believe on the Lord Jesus Christ and thou shalt be saved . . ." (Acts 16:31).

SCRIPTURES FOR MEDITATION
(Selah – think on these things)

MONDAY: *I am so glad for the Scriptures that hold the only true answer to the problem of immorality.*

Scriptures: Matthew 5:28-32; 1 Corinthians 7:1-2; Galatians 5:19-21; Ephesians 5:1-5; Revelation 21:8.

TUESDAY: *Lord, help me to not be naïve about evil, but at the same time not to allow it to have any place in my life.*

Scripture: Leviticus 18:22-30; Job 31:1; Romans 16:19; 1 Corinthians 6:15-20; Titus 1:15-16.

WEDNESDAY: *Lord, help me to not become complacent about evil, but to abhor it and grieve over it, even as You admonished Your people to do in the days of Ezekiel.*

Scriptures: Ezra 10:6; Nehemiah 13:25-27; Psalm 119:36-37; Ezekiel 9:4; 2 Corinthians 7:10.

THURSDAY: *Thank You Lord, for Your Word that tells me over and over that You do not condone sin in Your people. Help me walk in the cleansing power of the blood of Jesus!*

Scriptures: Romans 5:8-9; Ephesians 1:7; Hebrews 9:28; 1 Peter 2:24; 1 John 1:7; Revelation 12:11.

FRIDAY: *Lord, please protect the minds of our young people today. Let us be examples to them of how You want us to live.*

Scriptures: Deuteronomy 4:9; Philippians 3:17; 1 Timothy 4:12; Titus 2:6-8; 1 Peter 2:12-16.

SATURDAY: *Lord, no one can hide from You. You see all and someday all the secrets will be revealed unless cleansed by the blood of Your Son, Jesus!*

Scriptures: 1 Samuel 16:7; Proverbs 26:26; Ecclesiastes 12:14; Daniel 2:22; Matthew 10:26; Luke 8:17, 12:2-3; Romans 2:16.

Week 48

BUT WAIT, THERE'S MORE!

Our daughter Sandy just HATES commercials. In order to eliminate this annoyance, she records everything on her DVR. Pretty good idea you'll have to admit.

I also find most commercials quite annoying, but remember the Shamwow guy? Talk about funny. Watching him always brought a chuckle. I found myself saying, right along with him: "But wait. There's more!" I better start using my DVR more. I think I might be cracking up.

We have seen a multitude of these commercials. Bob Vila, best known for his advertising on American Home Improvement TV (This Old House – 1979-1989), held us spellbound as he would tout his latest product for sale. Just when you would think he was finished, he would dramatically point his finger at the TV audience and say, "But wait! There's more!"

Remember Ron Popeil. He used direct response marketing to push the collapsible fishing pole by Pocket Fisherman and he too, told us, "But wait! There's more!" There is even a card game called, "But Wait, There's More!" In the game the players pitch wacky products to each other for fun and profit. I think I might have to buy that game and quit playing so much Mexican Train. Sounds like a blast.

Figure 76 - Ron Popeil - But There's More!

With Easter now behind us, I just wanted you to hear this from me. "But wait. There's more!"

Things didn't end at the cross and the resurrection. Far from it; the disciples took that message to the ends of the Earth and now most of the world date events as B.C. (Before Christ) or A.D. (Anno Domini – Year of our Lord).

Remember Roma Downey from the hit TV series, Touched by an Angel? Roma and her husband Mark Burnett went on to produce one of the most watched TV series in history, The Bible.

According to one report the series received more than 100 million cumulative views. Not bad, I'd say. In addition to the large viewing audience, the series received three Emmy Award nominations for best miniseries, and sound editing and sound mixing on July 18, 2013. A feature film entitled *Son of God* developed from the series.

Figure 77 – Save Your Fork!

But wait! There's more! They also produced a sequel to the Bible miniseries, entitled, A.D. Downey stated, "A.D. chronicles the aftermath of Jesus' crucifixion as the tiny band of followers fight for survival as they spread the Word to the world. But they had hope and soon they had power: the amazing miracle of the resurrection and the arrival of the Holy Spirit upon them."

You can be sure I had my DVR set so I wouldn't miss this exciting series. The first episode aired Easter night on NBC (April 5, 2015).

In 2015 my sister, Star, held a memorial service for her daughter, Pam. Pam passed away at an early age, but she knew the Lord in a personal way. I'm sure if Pam could send a message back to us from Heaven she would say, "But wait. There's more! Don't mourn for me."

Once I heard of an elderly lady who wanted to be buried with her fork. Although that seemed rather curious, people didn't question her. It wasn't until the preacher spoke at her funeral that people finally understood the strange, last request.

The dear old saint had attended many church suppers in her lifetime. One thing she had always been told: "Hang onto your fork, honey. The best is yet to come." And sure enough, when the desserts came out she knew they were right.

As she planned for her Heavenly home she wanted folks to know that the best was yet to come and she was going to be ready. As she lay there in her casket there was a slight grin on her face. In her folded hands was a silver fork.

No matter how good you think things are now, the best is yet to come. No matter how bad things are looking, take heart: the best is yet to come. When people start to ask why you've started carrying a fork around with you, maybe you'll get a chance to say, "But wait. There's more! The best is yet to come."

SCRIPTURES FOR MEDITATION

(Selah – think on these things)

MONDAY: *I am so glad the "best is yet to come." Lord, please help me keep my eyes on the goal.*

Scriptures: 2 Chronicles 15:7; Psalms 20:7; Proverbs 3:5-6; Jeremiah 17:7-8; John 6:27-29; Philippians 3:13-14.

TUESDAY: *I am so grateful for modern technology. Today as never before the whole world can hear the Gospel via the modern means at our disposal. Help me do my part* *in supporting true ministries in spreading the Word of God.*

Scripture: Luke 6:38, 10:1-2; Romans 12:9-13; 2 Corinthians 2:15-17; Galatians 6:7-10; Hebrews 6:10.

WEDNESDAY: *I am so aware we are living in the last of the last days. Therefore, I will keep a sense of urgency about my witnessing. My words to others about Jesus might be the last words they ever hear before going into eternity.*

Scriptures: Acts 1:11; 1 Thessalonians 4:14-18; 2 Timothy 4:1-4; Titus 2:12-14; Hebrews 10:25.

THURSDAY: *Today, as never before, mankind will have no excuse when standing before God. I am so grateful for the many doors of opportunity God has opened. Lord, help me to walk through the doors before me.*

Scriptures: Genesis 3:11-13; Psalm 141:4; Luke 14:15-20; Romans 1:20; 1 Peter 2:16; 1 John 1:8.

FRIDAY: *It is so easy to criticize how others preach or teach. Help me Lord, to keep focused on what You want me to do and not what others are doing or not doing.*

Scriptures: Luke 6:37-42; Romans 14:1-4; Galatians 5:14-15; Colossians 3:12-15; James 4:1-12, 5:9.

SATURDAY: *When I think of those who have already gone ahead of me to glory. I am comforted, knowing they are enjoying the rewards of Heaven.*

Scriptures: Isaiah 25:8-12, 65:17; John 14:1-6; Colossians 3:1-4; Revelation 7:13-17, 21:4-7.

Week 49
ARE YOU SUPERSTITIOUS?

Some time ago, when our daughter lived in Florida, she was trying to rent a post office box. "Mom, the only number they have is 666. What should I do?"

I had to laugh because the post office was really having a hard time assigning that particular box and it certainly seemed it was because of the 666 number. At least that's what they told Dotty. (I'll let you decide whether she took the P.O. Box.)

Figure 78 - "666" - How did this Happen?

Last week I laughingly told a clerk that I was sure glad my total was off a few cents from being 666. I then turned around; standing behind me was a couple I knew quite well. They laughed too and said, "You might not believe this, but our daughter was born on 6-6-66." What? The clerk joined in the fun; said they needed to put her in a bag, tell them to take the baby back and bring them another one! We all laughed, but as I left the store I began to think about the difference between superstition and reality.

The dictionary definition of superstition is "a belief or practice resulting from ignorance, fear of the unknown, trust in magic or chance, or a false conception of causation."

The Bible gives us the true origin of the dreaded 666. In Revelation 13:16-18 John the Apostle writes: "He causes all, both small and great, rich and poor, free and slave, to receive a mark on their right hand or on their foreheads . . . the name of the beast, or the number of his name . . . his number is 666."

Although my friends and I joked about it, there is serious interest in the possibility of microchips being implanted in humans and animals. And if you think folks aren't interested in microchips, you might consider the following information.

There have been more than 31.7 million hits on Google's search engine for microchips; 25.8 million on Yahoo and 8.3 million on Bing. I would say there's quite a bit of interest on this subject. (For those not familiar with Google, Yahoo, and Bing, these are only a few of the Internet "search engines" available to obtain information on nearly every subject imaginable.)

There have been experiments in having a chip placed in your body for common everyday uses, such as turning on lights as you walk through the house or opening doors hands free.

Some chips may even have a GPS (Global Positioning System) in order to track people who are lost or to find prisoners who have escaped from a penal institution.

Back in 2003 Mexico's Attorney General, Rafael Macedo de la Concha and 160 of his deputies had microchips implanted in their arms, according to a report on NBC News.

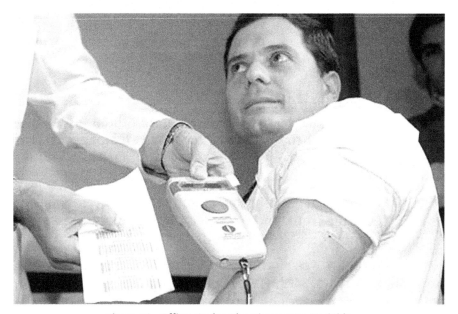

Figure 79 - Officer Carlos Altamirano Gets VeriChip

The reasoning for inserting the chips was "so only certain people could look at highly sensitive government material." Mexico is also using the chips as another tool in fighting the ongoing war on drugs.

According to news reports, "The microchip, about the size of a grain of rice, is injected under the skin and emits a low frequency radio wave. A scanner reads each chip's identification number to verify an official's security clearance."

Scott Silverman, of Applied Digital Solutions, whose company developed the futuristic chip, said, "The microchip is tamper proof; it's secure. No one can take your microchip and use it to their advantage to gain an access to your facility."

The microchips used in Mexico are similar to the ones now used in the U.S. to identify your pets and farm animals. In October 2004, the FDA approved Applied Digital Solutions of Delray Beach, Florida, to market the VeriChip for medical purposes.

When you think back about the dictionary definition of superstition, we who believe in the Bible as the plenary, inspired Word of God are not being superstitious when we tell people that 666 is a real number, for a real person.

It is superstition when we freak out if our sales receipt is $6.66 or when we refuse to allow the 911 office to give us a 666 address. Who knows, that might open a lot of doors of opportunity to talk about God's prophetic calendar to someone.

However, let me go on record here. If anyone tells me that I have to have a microchip implanted in me, saying its "mandatory," they just might have a fight on their hands. As Dotty and I used to say to each other: "First load. No chip!"

SCRIPTURES FOR MEDITATION
(Selah – think on these things)

MONDAY: *I am thankful that I know God will take care of me today and all the days to follow; therefore, I don't have to walk in fear.*

Scriptures: Psalm 118:5-6; Proverbs 3:21-24; Isaiah 12:2; John 14:27; Romans 8:15; Hebrews 13:6.

TUESDAY: *I totally reject all forms of witchcraft and superstition. Thank You Lord for freeing me from the bondages these things bring with them.*

Scripture: Deuteronomy 18:10-13; 1 Samuel 15:23; Isaiah 8:19-20; Micah 5:11-12; Acts 19:18-20.

WEDNESDAY: *I resolve, not only to be a serious student of the Word, but will share the things I've learned with others as the Lord opens up the doors of opportunity for me.*

Scriptures: Acts 17:11-12; 2 Corinthians 5:19-20; 2 Timothy 1:8; 1 Peter 3:15; 2 Peter 3:9.

THURSDAY: *I'm thankful that we can take the ordinary things that we see and hear on media outlets and use them as talking points in our witness to others.*

Scriptures: Psalm 19:1-6, 44:1-3, 68:11; Isaiah 40:28; John 9:24-34; Acts 26:19-29; Romans 10:13-17.

FRIDAY: *Lord, please let me not become conditioned to the looming evil that is coming upon the Earth. Help me remember that You are Sovereign and are still in control.*

Scriptures: Psalm 12:1; Micah 7:2; Matthew 24:12-14; Ephesians 5:16; 2 Timothy 3:1-17, 4:2-3.

SATURDAY: *Thank You Lord for the peace that I have in You. I am so thankful for Your presence in my life today.*

Scriptures: Isaiah 26:3; Matthew 11:28-30; John 14:27; Romans 14:17-19; Philippians 4:6-7.

Week 50
SEASONS OF LIFE

As we talked in the lobby of our local post office, my heart went out to my neighbor. His mother, only in her seventies, had just been diagnosed with Alzheimer's disease (AD). His life had suddenly, and radically, been changed by his mother's medical condition. Time had taken on a new perspective; work problems and job advancement didn't seem important anymore. All that mattered was spending time with his mother while she still knew him and could intelligently relate to him and his family.

My empathy, in part, was due to the fact that we had recently learned that my husband's eighty-six-year-old aunt was coming to live with us. Our lives, too, were taking a turn onto a new road. A road we have never traveled. It's one thing to have your elderly parents and relatives come for a visit, but when they've reached that final season in life and they're alone, needing someone; it's a different matter.

Figure 80 – Aunt Carrie Tuck

The letter had come just a few weeks before this meeting in the post office. "I want to come home," she began. Aunt Carrie had been with us during the previous summer and we had a wonderful time visiting with her. She loves church and being with caring people. It was neat, having this West Virginia mountain woman take over my kitchen, clean out my refrigerator and keep my laundry folded. Now she wanted to live with us on a permanent basis and I was wondering how I was going to keep my own identity as a housewife, while letting her feel free in taking over the meals and other household chores.

A visit was one thing . . . but a permanent resident?

Virginia, one of our youngest daughters chided me: "Remember Mom, the Bible says we're to take care of the widows and orphans."

Right! What if they can't see well enough to watch TV or read? What if they can't drive and need someone to take them everywhere? What if their health is failing because of a deteriorating disc?

Figure 81 - The Tuck Farm House in Georgia

Sandy, another daughter, jolted me by saying, "Hey Mom, don't forget . . . you'll be old like Aunt Carrie one day. You're just sowing for your old age, so you'll reap a good harvest."

Mercy me! Why did I teach those Scriptures to those kids of mine? I'm supposed to be preaching to them . . . not them to me! Then the Lord reminded me of a story I heard a long time ago.

Many years ago, in Asia, the younger would put the elder in a wheelbarrow and dump them over a cliff when their usefulness was over. On this particular day a little boy was following his father, as grandfather, looking sadly ahead, jostled back and forth in the wheelbarrow, aware of his soon coming fate. "Go home," the father sternly commanded the son.

Three times the command was repeated, and yet the little boy continued to follow his father, ignoring his instruction.

"Son," bellowed his father, for what was certainly the last time before judgment fell. "I am not telling you again. Why won't you listen to me and go home?"

Just as firmly, the little boy replied: "Father, I need to know where to take you, when it's your time to go." The father turned the wheelbarrow around and the three of them returned home.

You know it's amazing how your perspective can change overnight. What a fun time we had preparing for Aunt Carrie's stay with us. Charlie and I even drove thirty miles to a neighboring town just to pick up a little puppy that would keep her company during the day while we were at work.

Friend, have you had to readjust your schedule to bring blessing to an elderly or sick relative? Has your lifestyle been cramped a bit because of a change in your family situation? Perhaps you've had to help an adult child who has gone through a divorce and they need to get their life together. Your children are grown, but now you find yourself raising grandchildren.

Now let's see . . . I have eight children . . . if I work this just right . . . in my old age, I could live with each of my kids for about a month and a half each year, (sure hope none of them will expect me to clean out their refrigerators like Aunt Carrie did for me) and as for cooking . . . .

SCRIPTURES FOR MEDITATION

(Selah – think on these things)

MONDAY: *I will trust You Lord to keep my mind keen and sharp throughout all my days.*

Scriptures: 1 Chronicles 28:9; Nehemiah 4:6; Isaiah 26:3; Mark 12:29-30; Romans 12:2; 2 Timothy 1:7.

TUESDAY: *May our home always be used to bring blessing to others.*

Scripture: Romans 12:6-13; Colossians 3:23-24; 1 Timothy 5:9-10; Hebrews 13:16; 1 Peter 4:8-10.

WEDNESDAY: *Each day I am making an investment into eternity. I pray as I enter into the last stages of this life, that I will be prepared for the next.*

Scriptures: Job 14:14-16; Psalm 39:4-7; Proverbs 23:4-5; Luke 12:35-40; James 4:13-17, 5:1-5.

THURSDAY: *I will be mindful that my actions can influence others for good or bad. Lord, please help me to be a good example today.*

Scriptures: Romans 12:1-2; 1 Corinthians 10:31; Ephesians 5:1-2; 2 Thessalonians 1:10-12; Titus 2:7.

FRIDAY: *I cannot change my past, but I can make a difference in my future by the choices I make.*

Scriptures: Deuteronomy 30:19-20; Isaiah 30:21; Matthew 7:13-14; Galatians 6:7-8; Philippians 4:8.

SATURDAY: *I will remember that unexpected changes that come my way may be the Lord's hand because I need spiritual refining. I will not balk at changes!*

Scriptures: Psalm 33:10; Luke 1:1-26, 5:19; Acts 19:9-20; Romans 8:28; 1 Thessalonians 5:18.

Week 51

UNSEEN FOOTPRINTS

She was totally engrossed in reading her bible as she waited for the mechanic to finish working on her car. Bob Allen, a friend from Cochran also waiting for his car to be repaired, said, "Excuse me Ma'am; do you read the bible a lot?"

Pleased that he had opened a conversation, she proceeded to tell him that her husband had recently died and her son was recovering from a serious auto accident. Despite these "seeming" tragedies, she was surprisingly upbeat. She let Bob know that, in her opinion, God was a still a good God. Even though she didn't understand why her family had been going through these trials, she knew He would take her through. Even though she couldn't "see" Him, she knew He was there.

As Bob shared that incident with me I thought of the scripture in Psalm 77:19, "Your path led through the sea, Your way through the mighty waters, *though Your footprints were not seen.*" The Psalmist was describing the triumph of the children of Israel, who had passed through the Red Sea in victory!

We cannot always "see" the footprints, but He is there. Charlie and I have faced many Red Seas in our 44 years of marriage. Space and time will not permit me to go into detail, but suffice it to be said, God has been faithful.

Figure 82 - Bob Allen

Years ago, our daughter Linda had to have a routine surgery and during the process the surgeon accidentally cut a main artery, causing her to lose over a liter of blood. It was only after the surgery was completed that we learned she could have lost her right leg . . . or her life.

For several days we had maintained a vigil over her in the intensive care unit. Prayers were sent up on her behalf by friends from all over the world. And God answered . . . in His way . . . and she is still here. God is so good and He would have still been good even if He had taken her home. We are learning, day by day, month by month, year after year, that no matter what happens we serve a good God.

Figure 83 - Footprints in the Sand

We can say . . . He is good . . . even though one time Charlie broke his right knee and sprained his left ankle at the same time! He has been good when I faced frustrations in juggling my job with my responsibilities as a wife, mother, and grandmother. He has been good when my mother-in-law was rushed to the hospital with a severe breathing problem and it was impossible for us to consider making a trip to West Virginia because Charlie's leg was in a cumbersome cast. God is good at all times and in every situation.

Someone said, "Life is hard, and then you die." That is the world's view. The Christian view goes like this: "To live is Christ . . . and to die is gain."

Because sin came into the world, the resultant effects plague us. People are stricken with disease, children die tragically; fires, earthquakes, and hurricanes bring devastation and good people suffer in a million ways. Why? If God is good, what is the answer to these "seeming" inconsistencies?

He led . . . and His footprints were not seen.

Can God actually be leading us when we experience hard times? Can good people, church going folks, who are sincere and love God, suffer adversity? Absolutely!

In one of the hardest to understand books in the Bible, we find a true servant of God experiencing the ultimate in tragedies. All of Job's children are wiped out as they are having a get together at one of the sibling's home. Job's livelihood and his possessions are devastated when thieves steal and destroy everything he owns. Finally, we see him sitting on an ash heap, scraping his boil covered body with a piece of broken pottery. His wife and friends are quick to accuse him of sin, while he's in this pitiful state. Down through the ages we hear his agonizing cry: "Better to have never been born than to experience all these trials."

Yet, life went on for Job. After this terrible trial, he lived another 140 years, experiencing restoration in every area. Through it all he had maintained his belief in a Redeemer who would one day stand upon the earth. He believed he would see his children again. He endured as seeing Him Who is invisible.

Today, God is leading. Though we cannot see His footprints, He is there! Don't despair, child of God. He will get you through your Red Sea. He will bring you safely to the other side, and when you look back you will say: "His footprints led me all the way!"

SCRIPTURES FOR MEDITATION

(Selah – think on these things)

MONDAY: *Lord, please help me share words of comfort and encouragement to those who are going through difficult times.*

Scriptures: Psalm 31:24; Proverbs 12:25; Isaiah 43:2; John 14:27, 16:33; 2 Corinthians 1:3-6; 1 Thessalonians 5:11.

TUESDAY: *Lord, I am thankful You are there for me whenever I am going through various trials and temptations.*

Scripture: Deuteronomy 7:19-21; 1 Samuel 26:24; Acts 20:19-24; James 1:1-3; 1 Peter 1:6.

WEDNESDAY: *I know that whatever happens in my life that God has allowed it and it will work for my good and God's glory.*

Scriptures: 2 Chronicles 15:7; Isaiah 55:8-9; Romans 2:7, 5:3, 8:28; Hebrews 10:36; James 1:2-3.

THURSDAY: *I determine to keep my trust in the Lord when things happen that I have no control over. He will perfect all that concerns me because God is love!*

Scriptures: Deuteronomy 7:9; Psalm 86:15, 136:26; Zephaniah 3:17; John 3:16; Romans 8:37-39.

FRIDAY: *I refuse to accept words of condemnation, whether those words come from people, the Devil, or even words of self-condemnation. I am free of all condemnation!*

Scriptures: Psalm 34:22; Isaiah 50:9; Zephaniah 3:15; Romans 8:1; John 3:17, 8:11; 1 John 3:21.

SATURDAY: *I refuse to blame God for the results of my own bad decisions. I will confess my sins and receive His forgiveness and go forward!*

Scriptures: Deuteronomy 24:16; Ezekiel 18:20; 2 Corinthians 5:10; Galatians 6:5; 1 Timothy 5:8.

Week 52
WRITING OUR AUTOBIOGRAPHY

In 2002 one of Hollywood's greats passed away. Charlton Heston, who appeared in at least 60 films, was not only a movie star but also served seven terms as president of the Screen Actors Guild. In his later years he was an outspoken conservative on the political scene and served as president of the National Rifle Association from 1998 to 2003.

I remember being so saddened to learn of his battle with Alzheimer's disease. At that time he said, "For an actor there is no greater loss than the loss of his audience," he continued, "I can part the Red Sea, but I can't part with you . . . ."

His reference to the Red Sea was familiar to those of us who saw him play the part of Moses in the 1956 movie, *The Ten Commandments*. Although his family has not shared the actual cause of Heston's death, there is no doubt the Alzheimer's disease was a contributing factor.

Today, according to the Alzheimer's Foundation, it is the sixth-leading cause of death in the United States. As many as 5.5 million Americans are living with this disease. Alzheimer's Disease (AD) destroys brain cells, causing problems with memory, thinking, and behavior. AD gets worse over time, and it is fatal.

Like most movie stars and other celebrities, there are always those who, or so it seems, are there to write about their lives. I'm sure Heston had many biographers working on compiling the events of his life. Perhaps he even wrote his own autobiography in his later years before AD robbed him of his memory and cognitive functions.

One of my deepest regrets is that I did not record the many stories my own father shared about his life, before his passing with AD. Determined not to lose our family's stories of life in Georgia, Charlie and I wrote a little book for our children and grandchildren about our early days in Georgia and gave them out as Christmas presents one year. Hopefully, now that

I'm retired, I'll compile more recollections for the Tuck's future generations.

Figure 84 – Wedding Day with Jerri's Parents

Where would we be today without the compilation of the wonderful stories in the Bible? The greatest biographies of all are written in the Word of God and continue to bring blessing after blessing as we read and reread.

This week I have been so challenged while reading the life of Daniel and his three friends, Shadrach, Meshach, and Abednego. Their courage and determination to live for the Most High God are such an inspiration. (Daniel 1-6)

Who could tire of reading about Moses, Joshua, and Esther? Also, when I think of John the Apostle, who walked with Jesus and then ultimately wrote the fascinating book of Revelation, I am inspired to press forward.

This past year Charlie and I have been enjoying a book written by Robert J. Morgan in our morning devotions. The book is a compilation of stories of faith from 20 centuries of church history. Most of the people we have never heard of, but they are known to God.

Today you are living a chapter in the biography of your life. Have you taken time to write it down? We may not be as famous as Charlton Heston, but our lives are important to the Lord and to those who love us. Don't let the stories die. Pass them on to the generations to come.

And . . . since this is the last week in the **JUST JERRI** devotional book, I want to say it has been a wonderful year with you! I pray the declarations, prayers, and Scriptures have inspired you to live for God and that you will share your own stories with others, especially your family. My sincere prayer for you is that the Lord will bless and keep you and cause His face to shine upon you in all you do for His glory and honor!

Figure 85 – Autobiography for Tuck Kids

SCRIPTURES FOR MEDITATION
(Selah – think on these things)

MONDAY: *I will never forget those who paved the way for me in my walk with the Lord. I will always honor their memory.*

Scriptures: Psalm 116:15; 1 Thessalonians 5:12-13; Hebrews 13:7-8; Revelation 14:13.

TUESDAY: *I'm so grateful the Word of God has been preserved down through the ages. I will not take the Bible for granted, but read it every day.*

Scripture: Joshua 1:8; Nehemiah 8:3; Job 23:12; Romans 10:17; 2 Timothy 3:16-17.

WEDNESDAY: *The authenticity of the Bible has been proven over and over through scientific and archaeological proofs. I am so glad I can depend on God to stand by His Word.*

Scriptures: 2 Samuel 7:28; Psalm 19:9, 119:160; John 8:32, 17:17; Revelation 21:5.

THURSDAY: *Although I have never met those saints of old who gave their lives for God and His Word, I am assured I will meet them one day in Heaven.*

Scriptures: Matthew 17:1-8; 22:31-32; Hebrews 11:32-40, 12:1-2; Revelation 6:9-11, 22:1-5.

FRIDAY: *Lord, please help me to leave a spiritual legacy for my children and their children. May they remember that I loved You and that my prayer for them has been that they would join me in Heaven one day!*

Scriptures: Acts 16:31; Romans 1:9; 2 Corinthians 5:8-10; Ephesians 1:16; Philippians 1:21-24.

SATURDAY: *I will be committed to the charge God has given me to put Him first in all things and seek nothing but His glory in my life!*

Scriptures: Deuteronomy 4:29; Psalm 27:4-8, 40:4-8, 63:1; Matthew 6:31; Romans 2:7.

**THE TUCK KIDS
DOWN ON THE FARM**

Written by Grandma Tuck
Edited by Grandpa Tuck

December 24, 2003

Table of Contents

Special Letter

Chapter 1 ....The Beginning

Chapter 2 ....Romance at Sly Park

Chapter 3 .... A Wedding to Remember

Chapter 4 ....Life Together Starts With A Boom!

Chapter 5 ....Moving to Georgia

Chapter 6 ....This Old House

Chapter 7 ....Animal Farm

Chapter 8 .... Family Reunions

Chapter 9 ....Homegrown Love and Produce

Chapter 10 .... A Garden of Prayers

Chapter 11 ....Farm Kids Have Fun Too

Chapter 12 ....Hunting, Working and Driving

Chapter 13 .... A Night to Remember

Chapter 14 .... Christmas Tradition

Appendix .... Poems, Songs, Recipe

Figure 86 – So Many Stories Preserved

ABOUT THE AUTHOR

Jerri Tuck has served her Lord with passion and fervor since accepting Christ in February of 1957. In her B.C. days she rode with the notorious Hell's Angels motorcycle gang in California. A dramatic encounter with Jesus in a home Bible study changed the direction of her life.

Figure 87 - Charlie & Jerri Tell Their Story

In her secular career she has been a disc jockey with radio station WVMG, a feature writer and reporter for the Macon Telegraph & News, and a successful real estate broker and appraiser for 28 years. Since 1997 she has written a weekly column entitled *Just Jerri*, for which this book is named.

Immediately after her conversion experience in 1957, Jerri began to serve the Lord, working as a teacher with Child Evangelism Fellowship, and eventually became a trainer of teachers. Hundreds of boys and girls came to salvation through her outreach in weekly Good News Clubs from California to Pennsylvania.

Her foreign mission work has included missionary trips to Brazil, India, Ecuador, Mexico, China, Costa Rica and working for a Jewish organization (Ser-El), volunteering to help the Israeli Defense Force (IDF) in Israel.

Shortly after moving from California to Georgia in 1974 she became involved with the Women's Aglow Fellowship International. From holding monthly Aglow meetings in her hometown of Cochran, she became the president of the Central Georgia Women's Aglow Area Board.

On August 6, 2004 Jerri was honored at a special ceremony in San Antonio, Texas as one of only 17 women throughout the world in the Church of God in that year, to be inducted into the Hall of Christian Excellence through the COG Women's Ministries.

Earlier in 2004 Jerri started the first Bible Reading Marathon in the state of Georgia through the International Bible Reading Association. This has continued every year since, and has been spreading to other counties in Georgia.

Jerri is currently serving on the board of the Bleckley Christian Learning Center (BCLC) and is also a substitute teacher for the organization. BCLC just completed their first year of holding Bible classes in the Bleckley County public school system. She is also secretary for the Cochran-Bleckley Ministerial Alliance, RSAT Coordinator for all the Christian meetings held at a local detention center and teaches Sunday School at New Life Church of God in Cochran.

Jerri has written a challenging book about evangelism entitled *Gone Fishin'* and another book of the personal journey of her blended family, entitled *Patchwork Family*.

When God said, "Who will go?" her response was immediate . . . "Here am I, Lord. Send me."

(Jerri and her husband Charlie have been married 44 years. They have 9 children, 21 grandchildren and 11 great-grandchildren. They make their home in Cochran, GA. Charlie was the Chief Appraiser for Bleckley County and is also retired.)

To contact Jerri:

Go to her FaceBook page:

www.facebook.com/jerri.tuck.75

or email her at:

jerrituck@aol.com

Figure 88 - The Cochran Journal, Cochran, GA

Other Books by Jerri Tuck

From the very first day I became a Christian deep down I knew the answer to three questions. 1. Where did I come from? 2. Where am I going? 3. Why am I here? That inner knowing of the answers to these three perplexing questions propelled me into the world of "fishing for men." This little book, *Gone Fishin'*, is now in its third printing and has been used to bless and encourage those struggling with "How to reach people with the Good News of the Gospel?" It has brought hope and salvation to those who were sinking into an abyss of despair.

I'm just an ordinary person who strives to be in tune with an extraordinary God. Just as Peter and John were considered unlearned and ignorant fishermen, I have qualified to fish for souls, despite my ignorance, because of Jesus. My credentials are nothing to brag about, but I know I have bragging rights about the Savior who rescued me.

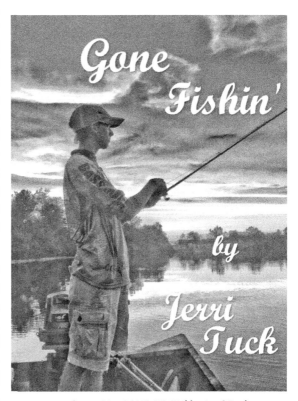

Figure 89 - GONE FISHIN' by Jerri Tuck

In these chapters you will find people just like the ones you rub shoulders with every day. In my case I owned a small real estate company in rural Georgia and God turned it into a soul-saving station.

Just Jerri

You will read accounts of professionals who, under their sophisticated facades, were bankrupt and miserable. You'll discover how they learned the true meaning of life and how they became more successful than they ever dreamed.

You'll also read about those who were living deviant lifestyles, not realizing God had a better plan for them; a plan that included freedom from sin. You'll drive down a rutted road with me and see Ted who had been living in an abandoned bus. Then you'll ride with me to a truck stop and wait with me while Ted takes a shower, his first one in six months. You'll see how God's love poured out to him and others and brought them to salvation. Fishing for souls is the most exciting vocation a person can have.

It's a job you won't find advertised on a computer employment site, or in a classified ad in your local newspaper; yet, it is a vocation you can couple with any other job you have. In my case it was a man who owned a pest control company who brought my whole family to Christ. He actually began telling my family about Jesus while he was spraying for black widow spiders! Fishing for men is a command of our Savior, yet so few do it today. Most Christians seem to feel it's the preacher's job to go out and evangelize the lost. Evangelism is something we read about, but few ever become personally involved.

Is it any wonder that today we are losing the battle for the souls of men? By leaving this all-important work to a few professional preachers and a handful of TV evangelists we are missing the point of what Jesus has called us to do.

Whether you're a housewife, a garbage collector, a doctor or a teacher, God has called you (and me) to be fishers of men. This is not the work of only a select few. Every person, who calls themselves by the name of Jesus Christ, has a mandate to preach the Gospel.

"How then shall they call on him in whom they have not believed? And how shall they believe in him of whom they have not heard? And how shall they hear without a preacher? And how shall they preach, except they be sent? As it is written, 'How beautiful are the feet of them that preach the Gospel of peace, and

About the Author & Her Books

bring glad tidings of good things!'" (Romans 10:14-15—KJV)

Take time to read these adventures in soul winning. Try reading just one story each day. Soon, you too will be on your way to becoming a fisher of men.

Figure 90 - Cochran Journal's Stories on BRM

Just Jerri

My story could be told by thousands of others who have come from broken homes. Everything went topsy-turvy for me when I found my mother crying in the kitchen. The phone receiver was dangling from the wall and my mother was shaking her head from side to side, as deep sobs wracked her body.

My father had just called and told her he wanted a divorce. By the time my mother married my second step-father, I was well on the road to destruction. I secretly married at fifteen and shortly afterwards my husband was transferred overseas.

When my step-father discovered what I had done, he promptly kicked me out of the house; saying if I was old enough to be married I was old enough to be on my own. While my husband was overseas I led a double life.

On one hand, I kept writing to him and acting like the faithful wife, but in reality I was living with a man who, unbeknownst to me, was out committing robberies to support our lifestyle. During this time, my step-mother and father had become Christians. They were fervently praying that God would touch me and save me.

I'm so happy to tell you their prayers were answered. I would love to report that everything was perfect after I gave my heart to Christ, but such was not the case. After sixteen years of marriage, my husband left me for another woman.

In 1972 God brought a wonderful, godly man into my life. He has encouraged me to become the woman God designed me to be. My husband Charlie designed our wedding bands. Within a molded triangle are two initials: J.C.

This stands for Jerri and Charlie united in Jesus Christ. In 1979 I became a real estate agent—retiring 28 years later—it was a good fit for me. Well, what this is really all about is how God took me and my three children and Charlie and his 5 kids and decided to take all these different patches and make Himself a beautiful quilt—with all the imperfections neatly sewed together forming a beautiful quilt!

We even picked up one more kid along the way—Alan. I recently wrote *GONE FISHIN'* about winning souls to Jesus—but raising a patchwork family is the greatest challenge I could have ever faced—thanks to Jesus and my beloved Charlie, it all came together.

There are many so-called accomplishments along the way—but the greatest is by God's grace keeping home and hearth together in love. The story is still being written; and, yes, the circle has been broken but the quilt is still beautiful, as you will see.

Figure 91 - PATCHWORK FAMILY by Jerri Tuck

Made in the USA
Columbia, SC
29 March 2019